The **WORLD** at
WAR

igloobooks

Published in 2013
by Igloo Books Ltd
Cottage Farm
Sywell
NN6 0BJ
www.igloobooks.com

Copyright© 2013 Igloo Books Ltd

SHE001 0813
2 4 6 8 10 9 7 5 3 1
ISBN 978-1-78197-378-3

Written by Gerard Cheshire

Printed and manufactured in China

The WORLD at WAR

Contents

Interactive instructions

On your mobile, or tablet device, download the **FREE** Layar App.

Look out for the **SCAN WITH LAYAR** logo and scan the whole page.

Unlock, discover and enjoy the enhanced content.

SCAN WITH
layar
See page 5 for instructions

For more details, visit: **www.igloobooks.com**

Introduction

In many respects, the modern world has become defined by the two world wars. A century after the beginning of World War I, we now have the benefit of a hundred years hindsight to see just how things have been changed so much by worldwide conflict.

Perhaps the most obvious changes were technological. The arms race prompted by the desire to win the war, on both sides, meant that many areas of technology advanced dramatically during World War I (1914-18) and World War II (1939-45). The interwar period (1918-39) and the post-war period (1945-) have both seen marked technological progress for similar reasons. Even in the absence of conflict, the technological world war has continued unabated.

The areas of technological progress included transport (on land, through water and in air), communication (radio), computing (code breaking),

detection (sonar, radar and reconnaissance), ordnance (weapons and ammunition), medicine (antibiotics), materials (composites), energy (nuclear), propulsion (jets and rockets).

Just about every area of science, technology, engineering and manufacture was pushed forward by necessity. If it meant having an edge over the enemy, then it was usually worth the investment of time, effort, expertise and money

From a military point of view, advances in technology also resulted in a requirement for different strategic thinking. Battles on land and at sea were no longer a matter of meeting up and slogging it out until one side emerged the victor. It became necessary to work out ways of keeping the frontline dynamic and mobile, to avoid the stalemate of entrenchment. It also became necessary to figure out ways of invading coastlines from the sea and how best to utilize or defend against new phenomena, such as aircraft, tanks and submarines. The machines of war would come to dominate the battlefield as a defining characteristic of modern warfare.

There have also been great societal shifts, for the better, in terms of class structure and gender role. The deaths of so many men meant that traditional class structures were eroded and more women stepped into the shoes of traditionally male professions. There was also a fundamental change in the way humanity regarded itself, partly due to bewilderment at the destruction it had wrought upon itself as a single species. Also, there was utter shock at mans inhumanity to man, which betrayed an underlying animalistic nature that people had preferred to think was a trait lost in our prehistory.

On the international level, the world wars caused considerable changes to the political map. Ironically, the wars themselves had largely been about ambitions of territorial conquest, which were duly prevented, yet the movements of borders were considerable in the wake of conflict as the new world order was established. Empires fragmented, while new empires were created.

At the root of all of the horrific and wasteful bloodshed were concepts of difference between populations. The human ability to adopt varying beliefs, ideologies, philosophies, politics, ethics and morals is a defining characteristic of our species. To be so, it must have served an advantageous purpose in our distant evolutionary past, but the world wars demonstrated quite clearly that it now had the potential to make humanity destroy itself. Perhaps this is the most valuable lesson to have come from two global conflicts-that the human condition is flawed, because our future would be better served if we evolved psychological alignment and harmony.

British troops go forward in 'No Man's Land', Battle of the Somme, 1916

Gassed, inspired by John Singer Sargent's time on the front line; it depicts a side on view of a
line of soldiers being led along a duckboard by a medical orderly; their eyes are bandaged as
a result of exposure to gas and each man holds on to the shoulder of the man in front

WORLD
WAR ONE

British troops moving up to the
trenches, 2.5 miles East of Ypres

How the Trigger was Pulled

In the years prior to World War I, the political map of Europe was quite different from the present era. Some of the countries we know today were still evolving in terms of their territorial boundaries and ethnic tensions were running high in central and eastern regions.

At the heart of this area was the Austro-Hungarian Empire, which comprised lands that are now recognized as, all or part of, no fewer than fourteen countries. Naturally, the ethnic minority populations disliked having their lands held by the Empire and they disliked the regime of oppression placed on their peoples, from the Austrians and the Hungarians.

A Bosnian Serb, named Gavrilo Princip, had enough of living under the empirical thumb. He joined a nationalist paramilitary movement named the Black Hand, whose ambition it was to fight for Serbian independence.

In June 1914, Princip and his comrades learnt that the heir to the Austro-Hungarian throne, Archduke Franz Ferdinand, would be making an official visit to Sarajevo, so they hatched a plot to assassinate him in the name of their cause. On the 28th the Black Hand prepared to carry out their plan, but things went wrong and the Archduke escaped unharmed. However, following the visit his driver took a backstreet to avoid the possibility of a further attempt on the Archduke's life.

It just so happened that the dejected Princip was walking along that very same backstreet. He immediately seized his opportunity and shot both the Archduke and his wife at close range. The job was done, but Princip could not imagine the chain of events he had started by succeeding in assassinating the Archduke.

SCAN WITH
layar
**See page 5
for instructions**

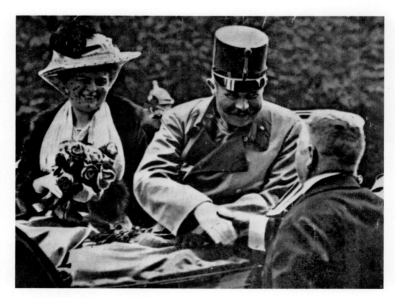

The Archduke and his wife, Sophie shortly
before their assassination in Sarajevo

Franz Ferdinand (1863 - 1914),
Archduke of Austria, heir-apparent
to the emperor Franz Joseph

The Austro-Hungarians wanted to take their revenge on the Serbian kingdom, amassed troops on the border and declared war. This prompted much political manoeuvring among the powers of Europe, according to historical allegiances. Just a month after the assassination, and the entire sub-continent was poised for war as all parties took their sides.

As for Princip, well he languished in prison for the next few years, where he eventually died from tuberculosis some months before World War I came to a close. His dream of an independent Serbia would not become a reality until the end of the 20th century and the region remains in a state of political tension due to ethnic divisions and political schisms. The Austro-Hungarian Empire was officially dissolved on the 31st October, 1918, eleven days before the official ceasefire of The Great War.

Serbian student Gavrilo Princip, who assassinated Franz Ferdinand

King Carol I of Romania from 1881.
At the beginning of World War I
he declared Romania neutral

Taking Sides

In the month following the Assassination of the Archduke Franz Ferdinand, the European nations took sides in preparation for all-out war, on a scale never seen before. The British Empire allied with the French and Russian Empires, to form the Triple Entente. The Austro-Hungarian Empire joined with the German Empire to form the Central Powers. Italy had initially agreed to join the Central Powers, but switched sides following the London Pact of 1915. The Italians had ambitions of building an empire, so the Entente promised them new territories as a reward for their allegiance.

A number of other European nations remained neutral, as they either had no vested interest in going to war, or they had no bellicose inclinations. They included the countries of the Iberian Peninsula, Scandinavia and South-eastern Europe. Serbia and Montenegro allied with the Russian Empire as part of the Entente. Switzerland remained neutral despite its being smack bang in the middle of the war zone.

Front page of French newspaper Le Petit Journal: Death to the Monster – France, England, Serbia, Russia and Belgium have declared war to Germany and Austria

As the key participants of the Entente and the Central Powers were empires, this meant that they each possessed territories and populations in other parts of the world. Although most of the fighting would take place in Europe, those involved were from a truly international collection of colonies, from all five continents. This is why it became known as the First World War, as opposed to The European War. Many described it as The Great War, until World War II superseded it in terms of scale.

Unfortunately, for the Central Powers, their combined empires were far smaller than those of the Entente, which immediately gave them a disadvantage, both in terms of material resources and available personnel. Despite the clear likelihood that they would ultimately lose the war, they chose to commence hostilities on the 28th July 1914. It seems that a combination of Teutonic pride and empirical ambition gave the enemy, who would widely become known collectively as the Hun or the Bosche, an over-inflated idea of their destiny, leaving them hell-bent on expanding their realm on the map of Europe and on the map of the World as a consequence of conquest.

The famous World War I recruiting poster featuring Lord Kitchener

A recruitment drive during the First World War at Trafalgar Square, London

Army recruits taking the oath at offices in White City, 1914

Blind Enthusiasm

A good deal of discussion has been conducted over the fact that most British soldiers volunteered to go to war in the initial stages. That is to say, conscription was not really required, because so many British men were enthusiastic about the idea of becoming soldiers and serving their country. So enthusiastic, in fact, that those considered too young to fight would often pretend to be older, and those considered too old would often pretend to be younger.

This blind enthusiasm seems to have resulted from a combination of factors in British society at that time in history. For one thing, very few people had first-hand experience of warfare in the Edwardian period, so most had little idea of the true horrors awaiting them. In addition, Britain was a rather staid and predictable environment, so the idea of adventure abroad was a very inviting prospect. There was also a strong sense of belonging to the great empire, so that men wanted to play their part in the war for fear of being seen of in a negative light by society.

British Army recruitment poster, 1917

It is also important to remember that there was a very clear class structure in Britain as a hangover from the Victorian era. The working class had laborious lives of subservience, repetition and drudgery. The middle class had tedious lives of pen pushing and managerial duties. The upper class had idle lives of hunting and sporting in imitation of true challenge. Not surprisingly, men from all three classes were excited by the prospect of donning uniforms and going overseas to give the enemy their dues.

In their minds it amounted to an adventure holiday, firing guns and enjoying a macho environment for a few months, before returning home with something to talk about for the rest of their lives. Very few seem to have had any real notion that there would be no more of their lives to enjoy. This was compounded by the propaganda used to invite them to war in the first place and the notion that warfare was no longer a matter of hand-to-hand combat, but rather something conducted over a civilized distance between friend and foe.

After eighteen months of fighting, the reality of modern warfare had become clear. So many men had been slaughtered on the killing fields that conscription was introduced for all men between the ages of 18 and 41 with the Military Service Act 1916. By 1918, the upper-age parameter had been raised to 51 years in order to compensate for the woeful losses on the Western Front. A young army had been all but replaced by a middle aged army.

Infantrymen sitting in a trench reading and smoking during the early days of trench warfare

British soldiers in the trenches during World War I, 1914

Entrenchment

When World War I broke out, on 28th July 1914, the Central Powers launched a campaign to reach the English Channel by advancing into France. This became known as the Race to the Sea and followed a number of opening battles in the war. These included the Battle of the Marne and the Battle of the Aisne. The original intention of the German Imperial Army had been to take Paris, but this ambition had been thwarted by the Allies, so the Germans tried a new tactic.

As the Germans tried to fight their way to the coast, the French and British forces resisted. Many subsequent attacks and counter-attacks eventually led to a stalemate situation in the region of Artois and Flanders. The result was a more-or-less static frontline between the opposing forces. So it was, that the Western Front became a north-south line, stretching from Nieuport in Belgium down towards Paris in France.

Due to the stasis, both sides were forced to settle into a prolonged trench war. Once in a while, offensives and counter-offensives would move the frontline westward and eastward, but never any considerable distance. This meant that the same swathe of fighting terrain was occupied for about four years. As a consequence, the landscape became a featureless expanse of mud as hundreds of thousands of shells destroyed the trees and plowed the soil with their explosions. Buildings and roads suffered the same treatment, so that the battlegrounds became panoramas in shades of brown, with little to distinguish one place from another, save the odd ruin, tree stump, hill or stream.

German invasion of France: gray
hordes of infantrymen stream
forward relentlessly through the
peaceful sunlit fields of France

With every feature razed to the ground, it also meant nowhere to hide. The only option, for both sides, was to live a subterranean existence in trenches, tunnels and dugouts. Conditions were unpleasant to say the least. Not only did soldiers have to contend with unsanitary and damp conditions, but the land around them was strewn with the decomposing fragments of corpses. The winters brought constant muddy wetness and cold, while the summers brought the stench of putrefaction.

Then there were the animal pests to deal with: maggots and flies, hair and body lice, rats and mice. As eradication was impossible, the soldiers could only do their best to avoid infestations by keeping their environment relatively clean. Another serious problem was 'trench foot'. The footwear of soldiers allowed their feet to get damp and cold for prolonged periods of time. This resulted in swelling and secondary infections, which would lead to painful skin peeling and even loss of toes, rendering combatants unable to fight effectively.

British tommies relaxing and having wounds treated in an underground forward dressing station by the Menin Road in France

The Eastern Front

As the main Allied campaign was at the Western Front during World War I, it is often forgotten that there was also an Eastern Front. This is where the Russians, and their allies, took on the Austro-Hungarian army. Thus, the Central Powers had to fight on two flanks, in an effort to increase their empire both eastward and westward. Needless to say, it meant having to spread their resources with inevitable consequences in the long run.

At that time, Russia was in a state of political unrest and its infrastructure was not geared up to the material demands of war on this unprecedented scale. What it did have, however, was a vast population, so it was able to keep replenishing its battalions with new personnel. Nevertheless, the Russian people soon grew disillusioned by the sheer war effort and the enormously high casualty rate. To all intents and purposes, it felt as if the Russian monarchy was treating the war as if it were a giant game of chess, with human cost all part of the game.

Ultimately, this lack of concern for the common people led to revolution in February 1917. Tsar Nicholas was forced to abdicate and the Communist Bolsheviks took power, under the leadership of Vladimir Lenin. Having a new cause to fight for gave the Russian army a morale boost, putting the enemy forces on the back foot. Then the Communists attempted to cease hostilities with the Central Powers, but this resulted in a large-scale offensive from the enemy, sensing weakness in the Russian resolve, due to their own civil war.

Action in a British first line trench in the Balkans, Eastern Front

Adorned with flowers, a soldier of the Austro-Hungarian army prepares to leave for the Eastern Front

The Eastern Front finally fell peaceful in March 1918, with the Treaty of Brest-Litovsk. This enabled the Central Powers to divert their spare forces to the Western Front in the hope of finally winning the war. However, it was too late, as the US had declared war on Germany and begun sending troops to France and Belgium, thereby countering the additional manpower.

Unlike the Western Front, the Eastern Front was far more mobile, in both directions, which meant that trench warfare did not typify the theatre of war in that region. This had a good deal to do with the terrain, which was not generally flat and deeply soiled, but far more hilly and mountainous instead. As a result, offensives and counter-offensives moved the frontline considerable distances, as one force advanced and the other retreated.

German soldiers operating a
machine gun from a trench
on Russia's Eastern Front

American soldiers practising with
camouflaged artillery after their
arrival in France in 1917

Camouflage

It may be hard to believe, but in the initial stages of World War I, the French wore their traditional blue coats and red trousers on the battlefield. Needless to say, they stood out like sore thumbs against the greens and browns of the countryside and were easily targeted by the German riflemen, artillerymen and particularly the machine gunners. Before too long, the high command admitted that it might be better to give their troops a fighting chance, so they introduced a more neutral coloured uniform in grayish-blue, which was still pretty visible but a marked improvement.

The British had already learnt the value of mimicking the colours of battle terrain in the late 19th century, so they entered the war wearing uniforms in khaki, which is a drab, olive-green colour. Although khaki was a better colour than grayish-blue, both uniforms were still visible to one extent or another, because the background often comprised many hues and tones. Textile technologies were not able to produce the complex patterns needed for more successful camouflage, but this realization led to rapid camouflage developments in other areas on the field of battle.

Machines of war, such as artillery guns, tanks and troop carriers were soon being painted in contrasting shades and colours, to obscure their outlines and make it more difficult for the enemy to interpret what they were seeing. These developments were accelerated by the introduction of aircraft into the theatre of war. As aircraft were able to view enemy activities from a vantage point, it became increasingly important to hide equipment and personnel. This resulted in the use of camouflaged canvas and netting for the purpose of concealment from above.

As the terrain at the Western Front was typically flat and featureless, it was very obvious if anyone so much as raised their head above the parapet, making reconnaissance rather dangerous. This led to the invention of artificial trees in the hope of gaining an elevated view without being shot. Steel-frame pylons would be hastily erected at night and then camouflaged with bark and foliage to look like shelled stumps. If the enemy had not noticed the change to the scenery the next morning, then it was possible to climb up the pylons and quickly survey the scene in the hope of gaining useful information.

A French soldier in his bright blue uniform, which made them easy targets amongst the green and brown landscapes

A German officer in a camouflaged position in a wooded area of the Vosges

British soldiers moving forward through wire at the start of the Battle of the Somme, 1 July 1916

Machine Guns

T
o many people, World War I is defined by a number of characteristics that set it apart from wars before and since. In particular, the entrenchment of troops on the Western Front, as both sides found it impossible to launch successful offensives on the flatlands of Belgium and France.

This circumstance arose due to the development of the machine gun and the terrain peculiar to that particular theatre of war. The Germans had a machine gun named the Maschinengewehr 08, which was based on an original design by Hiram Maxim, an American-born, British inventor. He had offered the gun to the British in 1884, but the British high command had not realized its potential. When the war broke out, the Germans already had 12,000 machine guns, and had 100,000 by the close of hostilities.

US soldiers of 23rd Infantry, 2nd Div. firing a 37MM infantry machine gun at a German position

It is generally agreed that a single machine gun was equivalent to around eighty riflemen, such was its rate of fire. As a consequence, it was virtually impossible to advance across open ground when faced with just one machine gun, let alone several. To make matters worse, the machine gun had such a concentration of fire that it was possible to have one's body cleaved in two by the stream of bullets.

Gas-masked men of the British Machine Gun Corps with a Vickers machine gun during the first battle of the Somme

A German machine
gun division with six
captured Russian guns
at Tirlancourt

Maxim's gun design utilized the exhaust gases of each preceding bullet to provide the energy required to load and fire the following bullet. This is why it was called a machine gun, and it was a simple and efficient design. It would fire at a rate of 300-600 rounds per minute, depending on how well maintained it was in field conditions.

The British, having failed to realize the advantages of the machine gun, had only a handful of old Maxim machine guns in 1914. By 1915, having suffered heavy losses, the British established its Machine Gun Corps, using a different design, called the Vickers machine gun.

Both, the Maschinengewehr 08 and the Vickers were heavy pieces of equipment, requiring a number of personnel to operate them. This meant that they were better used for defensive warfare, as they were not easily portable, as would be necessary for offensive operations. Eventually, assault machine guns came into use as the technology was developed sufficiently for lightweight designs. These included the Lewis machine gun, used by the allies, and the Bergman MP18 sub-machine gun, used by the Germans.

Soldiers of the 16th Canadian machine gun regiment using shell
holes as makeshift defences at Passchendaele Ridge

Shell Shock

In the Edwardian era, psychiatry was very much in its embryonic stage of development. This meant that the psychological symptoms of warfare were not tolerated, simply because they were not understood. These days, many soldiers are diagnosed with Post Traumatic Stress Disorder following combat, because the combination of long periods of anticipation followed by intense action and stress can have damaging effects on the nervous system.

During World War I, increasing numbers of troops began to suffer from nerve related behaviours, ranging from inability to face the enemy, to extreme reactions to noise, characterized by uncontrollable twitching and ticks. This became known as shell shock, and rendered many combatants disabled and unable to continue fighting. Prolonged exposure to the terror of shell fire, along with the sight of others blown to pieces, was too much for many to take, so their nervous systems closed down with alarming results.

In a way, it was better for those who displayed physical symptoms, as they were taken away to hospital for treatment, in the hope that rest and quiet might cure them of their afflictions. Those who developed lesser symptoms would often disobey orders or even run away to avoid subjecting themselves to further panic. This was interpreted as cowardice by commanding officers, who frequently had no first-hand experience of the horrors of frontline conditions. As a result, many were imprisoned and even shot as an example to others. Had the establishment had a better understanding of the neurological sciences, then they would have realized that these behaviours were involuntary.

Soldiers suffering from shell shock take up gardening to help them recover

English SE-5
single-seater plane
(top) and a German
Rumpler two-seater
in aerial combat on
the British front

War in the Air

As World War I began just ten years after the first flight of a powered aeroplane, it may seem remarkable that they were developed sufficiently to be useful machines in the theatre of war. However, their evolution had been rapid, because they captured the public imagination. Aviators were frequently setting themselves new challenges to see what their flying machines could do, and this resulted in accelerated progress. By the time the war had started, the aeroplane was reliable and had begun to take on the fundamental form upon which modern machines are typically designed.

Initially, aeroplanes were put to use for the purpose of reconnaissance over land and sea. As the Western Front was situated on such flat terrain it was virtually impossible to gain a vantage point without being shot. The aeroplane had the advantage of being able to fly out of gun range and above enemy-held territory, so that it was possible to take photographs of enemy positions. Needless to say, both sides had the same idea, so the aeroplane quickly adapted from an observation device to a machine of war, able to attack other aircraft and defend itself from their attentions too.

A French-built Nieuport XXIII
reconnaissance plane, circa 1916

Many biplane and monoplane designs appeared, as engineers tried to keep their machines ahead in the arms race. Having machine guns became a vital component of these warplanes, but propellers presented an obstacle to the passage of bullets. Some designs had twin engines, to allow the guns to be mounted in between. Some had pushing propellers, to allow the guns to sit in front. Others had rear-mounted gunners to defend against attack from the rear. Eventually, a mechanism was invented to allow the machine gun to fire through the rotating propeller blades, which meant that dog-fights became a feature of airborne warfare.

A common problem with these early aeroplanes was that they had very little payload. They were simply not powerful and fast enough to lift much additional weight off the ground. This meant there was no possibility of carrying armour plating, so aircrew were always vulnerable to being hit by bullets from other aeroplanes and from the ground. It also meant that the concept of the aeroplane as a bomber was only in its infancy when the World War I ended. The concept of the fighter, however, was well and truly established.

Before the Royal Air Force existed in Britain, military airmen either belonged to the Royal Flying Corps, as part of the British Army, or the Royal Naval Air Service, as part of the Royal Navy. By April 1918, the potential of military aircraft had been fully accepted and both forces merged to create the RAF.

German flying ace Heinrich Gontermann stands near his Fokker DR-1 tri-plane on an airfield, Germany

SCAN WITH
layar
See page 5
for instructions

British SE-5s locked in aerial combat, or dogfight, with German Fokker D7s

Belgian soldiers rush to commence battle,
on the banks of a canal near Ypres

Battles of Ypres

Fighting at the Western Front during World War I, was centred around a strategically important town, named Ypres, in West Flanders, which is a municipality of Belgium. During the course of the war, many offensives and defensives were fought along a frontline running roughly north-south. Although, there exact positions varied, many came to be known as the Battles of Ypres.

The first Battle of Ypres, in the autumn of 1914, established the pattern of trench warfare that would become synonymous with World War I. This was the result of some key factors. For one thing, many trained, regular soldiers perished in the hail of machine gun fire, so that they were replaced by volunteers. Also, reconnaissance information was lacking, which led to indecisive campaigns based largely on guesswork. As a consequence, both the Allies and the Germans found themselves losing personnel as quickly as they could be transported to the front, and a stalemate situation resulted.

In their individual shelters, on the front line, British soldiers, bayonet attached to their rifle barrel, await the German attack during the Battle of Ypres

Worst of all though, was the way in which the military was structured. The high command did not play an active role in the field. As a result, they kept sending lines of soldiers across no-man's-land, without appreciating that they were so easily cut down by enemy machine guns. Even though they were aware of such dreadfully high casualty rates, this lack of first-hand experience meant that it simply didn't impact them sufficiently to implement different tactics. The phrase 'going over the top' became part of the battlefield vernacular, as it was the command feared the most by the ordinary soldier, knowing it meant almost certain death. It also meant a pointless death, as it served no strategic purpose whatsoever.

Hundreds of thousands of Allies and Germans became casualties of war in Flanders, either killed, injured or missing in action. The exact numbers are not known, because records are imprecise. Astonishingly, nearly fifty thousand went missing during the Battles of Ypres. This is largely because they fell in no-man's-land and it was impossible to retrieve their corpses. Over time, shellfire either buried them or blew them to pieces, until there was no evidence of their having been there in the first place.

The endemic problem with the military high command's inability to empathize with the common man, was a result of the class structure in general society. Just as the Black Death caused a societal shift away from feudalism, due to the resulting lack of available manpower, so World War I would cause a similar societal shift away from the Victorian master-servant set-up. So, it can at least be said that the legacy of those who so needlessly died, was the initiation of a better society.

Stretcher bearers struggle in mud up to their knees to carry a wounded man to safety during the third battle of Ypres (Passchendaele)

British Soldiers in the Trenches during the Battle of Ypres in Belgium circa 1917

War at Sea

During World War I, warfare at sea played a significant factor, because it was all about supply of personnel and materials to and from other regions of the world. The Allies and the Central Powers both had substantial naval forces with which to do battle, but the Germans had developed the U-boat, which proved to be a particularly effective weapon against military vessels, merchant ships and troop carriers.

The U-boat (Underwater boat) was a class of submarine especially developed by the Germans for covert operations, able to fire torpedoes at the hulls of these craft with an element of surprise and devastation, which the Allies found difficult to counter. Sonar was yet to be invented and the British experimented with hydrophones in an effort to detect the engine noises of approaching U-boats with little success.

The role of the reconnaissance aeroplane became important as it was one of the best ways of detecting U-boats. It was then possible to alert shipping of their presence. The only effective way to counterattack U-boats was to drop depth charges and hope that the pressure waves would damage them sufficiently to either sink them or force them to the surface. For the most part though, it was better for cargo ships to travel in convoys, protected by military escorts. Until the introduction of escorts, U-boats had a field day sinking hundreds of supply ships bound for Britain and France from the US.

A British steamer is torpedoed, the picture was taken from the German U-Boat which has made the attack

Eventually the U-boats were rendered unable to sink sufficient numbers of Allied transport ships to have any serious effect on the supply chain to the frontline. The actions of U-boats against US warships also prompted the Americans to declare war on Germany, so the outcome of the war became inevitable.

As the U-boats are so well documented in history, it is often forgotten that the British had a number of World War I submarines of their own. They were primarily used in an effort to counter the U-boat threat, albeit with only limited success. The most numerous design was the E-class, of which 58 were launched between 1912 and 1916. They were also used to lay mines across shipping lanes used by the enemy and to assist in campaigns where troops needed to be delivered to coastal regions.

A U-boat opens fire with a deck cannon, on an allied merchant ship

The interior of a British E class submarine, 1916

Tanks

The Battle of the Somme was the first theatre of war in which a tank was used. The stalemate situation of trench warfare had arisen due to a peculiar combination of traditional tactics and advancing technology, which meant neither side was able to move forward in any decisive way. The idea behind the tank was simply a means of traversing the battlefield without being mown down by machine gun fire. It was a case of necessity being the mother of invention.

The first tanks were, however, only prototypes, as the Battle of the Somme was effectively

their testing ground. They were unwieldy and unreliable, so that operators found them difficult to manoeuvre-especially under heavy fire-and would often find themselves stranded in no-man's-land, unable to restart their engines. In addition, they had poor visibility and limited effectiveness in terms of their own ability to return fire. This was because they had not yet adopted the standard tank format, with a rotating turret mounted above the traction unit. Instead, they had guns mounted to the side, between the track rails.

First World War tanks were descendants of vehicles like this early caterpillar-track farm machine

In short, tanks were primitive and poorly designed. As a concept though, their potential was clear enough, as they did indeed protect their occupants and they protected troops who used them as moving shields. In addition, they had a significant psychological effect on the enemy, who feared being crushed to death by the cumbersome machines as they trundled blindly over trenches and dug-outs.

The idea of the tank came from a British soldier named Ernest Dunlop Swinton. A friend had mentioned that an armoured tractor might be useful at the front, so Swinton began to think about ways of combining the basic concept of the track-propelled tractor, which had only just been invented, with a capacity to carry artillery.

The name 'tank' came about simply because the first machines were nothing more than mobile metal tanks. This early format, without the familiar gun turret, arose because the available technology was limited and it made sense to have everything contained within a single chamber and with a low centre of gravity.

By the close of World War I, the tank had begun to evolve rapidly. Ironically, it was the Germans who recognized its true potential and subsequently perfected its design between the wars. In 1940 the Panzer tanks used by the Germans, in their Blitzkrieg of Western Europe, were state-of-the-art machines that destroyed the tanks available to the Allies.

The German A7V tank, created by Daimler-Benz, weighed 26 tons and had a top speed of 12km/h; it carried a crew of up to 18 men

An American soldier walks ahead of an MKIV British-made tank, 1918

Zeppelins

Rigid airships, or dirigibles, were conceived in the late 19th century and the first flight took place in 1900, preceding the first powered aeroplane flight by three years. The name Zeppelin became synonymous with airships because it was the German pioneer Count Ferdinand von Zeppelin who got the idea off the ground, quite literally. Unlike hot air balloons, which relied on hot air being less dense than cold air, Zeppelins relied on the relative density of gases. They were filled with the lightweight gas hydrogen, which was less dense than the combination of gases in the atmosphere.

As Zeppelins could be made very large, it meant that they could carry considerable payloads, making them perfect for transporting passengers and their luggage. They could also be propelled with engines

and piloted, again unlike hot air balloons, so that regular services were established. Inevitably, the German military saw great potential in Zeppelins when World War I broke out. Zeppelins were ideal for scouting missions and for bombing the enemy.

They had a few drawbacks, as they were ill-suited to operating in windy weather conditions and hydrogen is highly flammable, taking only a spark to set it alight, but aeroplanes were simply not advanced enough to do a better job at that stage in history. So, Zeppelins were used extensively by the Germans, especially in situations that required prolonged reconnaissance work, such as detecting warships in the Baltic and North Sea. Aeroplanes simply did not have the range or fuel capacity to remain airborne for long enough.

The Army airship Beta II at Aldershot, 1915

Wrecked houses at St. Peter's Plain, Yarmouth
after a Zeppelin bombing raid, January 1915

The gondola of a German airship

A newspaper vendor in a London street announces the news of a Zeppelin raid on England

Zeppelins were even used for bombing raids over Britain, which came as quite a shock in a world coming to terms with the possibilities of flight in general. A number of east coast towns, cities and docks were targeted with success, not least because Britain was yet to implement a strategy against air raids. By 1916 many anti-aircraft guns and searchlights were positioned on British territory to counter the Zeppelin threat. In truth, the bombing raids did relatively little damage in material terms, but their psychological effect was considerable as no one had imagined that they might be in danger in their own homes when the frontline was hundreds of miles away in France.

This also called into question, whether it was ethically acceptable to bomb civilians. Inevitably, British sentiment towards the Germans grew increasingly negative, although the Kaiser did initially order that primary targets should be places of strategic value and that bombing in an indiscriminate manner simply to terrorize was to be avoided. As the war progressed, such considerations went out the window, and Zeppelins increasingly dropped bombs and incendiaries where they could. City defences improved however, so the airships began to target less densely populated places.

Belgian gun crew at work during
the Siege of Antwerp, 1914

A German L21 Zeppelin sinks off
the coast of Yarmouth, Norfolk,
after having been shot down

Artillery

Trench warfare made rifles, pistols and machine guns relatively ineffective at reaching the enemy, unless they happened to attempt an assault or were foolish enough to expose themselves to gunfire. This meant that other field weapons were increasingly relied upon to strike at the unseen enemy. These weapons characteristically had parabolic trajectories so that the projectile came down from above and hopefully fell into enemy trenches.

The handheld grenade was designed for this very purpose, as it could be lobed in an arc, but it required the soldier to be near enough for the grenade to reach the target. This was virtually impossible as the soldier would need to leave his own trench and traverse no-man's-land to be within range. As a result, the mortar was developed, which was basically a mechanically assisted grenade. It was ejected from a launch tube and was capable of travelling several hundred yards.

Belgian soldiers make a charge near the River Yser

Next on the scale were the field guns. They were capable of firing exploding shells over several miles distance, so they were stationed a long way behind the frontline in order that their ammunition fell on the enemy at the correct angle to do maximum damage. Needless to say, the room for error was considerable, so accurate sighting adjustments relied greatly on reconnaissance information. Even then, the targeting could be quite arbitrary, so the big guns kept firing until they had given the whole area a good pounding. Of course, it was also possible to be hit by friendly fire, if the artillerymen set their guns with too short a range.

The most frequently used artillery were howitzers. They were short barrelled guns that fell somewhere between mortars and field guns in terms of their firepower and their trajectory. They were also relatively lightweight and mobile, making them ideally suited to being moved about behind the field of battle. As howitzers were designed to fire ammunition over relatively short distances, at high trajectories, they were capable of delivering shells twice the size of those delivered by equivalent field guns.

The combination of the steep angle of attack and large shell size made them formidable weapons when they hit target. If a battery of howitzers launched a simultaneous attack, then whole areas containing enemy positions could be obliterated in minutes. The aim was to breach the enemy's frontline in this way, so that offensives could quickly be launched before the enemy had time to recover and defend themselves. This usually worked for only short periods of time, so that the Western Front changed shape here and there, but essentially remained in the same place year after year.

Three 8-inch howitzers of 39th Siege Battery, Royal Garrison Artillery (RGA), firing from the Fricourt-Mametz Valley during the Battle of the Somme

British troops hauling a gun
into position under cover
of a ridge at Salonika

Chemical Warfare

O nce the Allies and the Germans had settled into trench warfare on the Western Front it marked a sea-change in the strategic psychology of those orchestrating the warfare. Realizing that conventional weapons were failing to break the deadlock they got to thinking about new technologies that might make a difference. This led to the unfortunate use of gaseous chemicals in efforts to incapacitate large numbers of the enemy while they languished in their trenches, foxholes and dug-outs.

The first gas to be used in this way was chlorine. The Germans used it against the Allies at the Second Battle of Ypres in 1915 and the British were quick to retaliate. However, the dispersal of gas requires a favourable wind and the British ended up gassing their own troops. Chlorine is an extreme irritant when inhaled, because it reacts chemically with water to produce hydrochloric acid and hypochlorous acid. Relatively few victims of chlorine gas died, but they were rendered unable to fight for considerable periods of time. In addition, chlorine gas was visible and odorous, so that it had a detrimental psychological effect on soldiers when they realized a cloud of the gas was coming their way. As it was heavier than air, it would creep along the ground and pool into low-lying places, forcing troops to evacuate their hiding places and expose themselves to enemy fire.

British casualties blinded by mustard gas in a German gas attack at Bethune, France

Two US soldiers wear gas masks while walking through plumes of smoke, 1917

Gassed and blinded French infantrymen are led by comrades, and
escorted by British soldiers from the second Battle of the Marne

The second gas to be used in World War I was
phosgene, which is a compound of chlorine with
oxygen and carbon. Unlike chlorine, phosgene was
invisible and virtually odourless, making it more
effective at poisoning the enemy, because they found
it more difficult to detect. Its effects were more lethal
too, although it took some time before the necessary
chemical reactions had taken place. The phosgene
molecules prevented the lungs from absorbing
oxygen, so the victim died from asphyxia.

The third gas was mustard gas, which was also a
compound of chlorine, with sulphur, carbon and
hydrogen. Mustard gas killed far fewer soldiers than
phosgene, but it became far more notorious due to
the unsightly and painful blistering it caused on
contact with the skin and airways. Mustard gas was
used extensively by the Central Powers against the
Russians on the Eastern Front.

Various gas masks with chemical filters were
developed to counter the effects of these gases, but
mustard gas proved more difficult to deal with due
to its vesicant properties, which rendered soldiers
inoperative even if they managed to avoid inhaling it
or being blinded by it.

French troops wearing an early
form of gas mask in the trenches
during the 2nd Battle of Ypres

Flamethrowers

One of the drawbacks with using chemical weapons at the Western Front was that the lingering gases would often make it hazardous for troops to advance, even if their gas attacks had been successful. As a result, military engineers were tasked with devising other ways of flushing the enemy from their trenches. This led to the development of the flame thrower. It was essentially nothing more than a stream of burning flammable liquid pumped under high pressure towards the target.

In places where the enemy was close by, the flamethrower proved quite effective at filling trenches with flames so that the occupants had no option but to evacuate into the line of fire of rifles and machine guns. Incredibly, in some parts of the frontline opposing trenches were fewer than five metres apart, but typically they were separated by a swathe of no-man's-land measuring more than fifty metres. This presented a problem for flamethrowers, because they were not yet portable, so their range was limited by the distance the fuel could be thrown. As a result, engineers dug tunnels beneath no-man's-land so that it was possible to emerge closer to the enemy and surprise them with a shower of flames.

One of the first flamethrowers used by the French against an enemy trench

Austrian soldiers on the Eastern Front preparing to throw burning liquids

A British tank burns furiously, having been caught in
the jet of a flamethrower and its fuel contents ignited

The Germans made extensive use of semi-portable
flamethrowers during World War I, as they
were effective at intimidating the enemy and so
preventing them from advancing. The most ambitious
flamethrowers were built by the British. They were
called Livens flame projectors and were so big that
their use was only intended to be part of the shock
tactics in launching effective offensives. Five are
known to have been made, but only three were put
to use. Two saw action in the Battle of the Somme,
sending enormous jets of flame from no-man's-land
prior to troop advances. They probably achieved
little in terms of actually killing the enemy, but they
certainly struck fear into the hearts of the Germans,
for it is known that fewer Allies perished at the points
where the flamethrowers were deployed.

The designer, William Livens, also engineered a wide-
bore mortar, called the Livens Projector. It was used
to fire large canister bombs containing flammable
liquids and toxic chemicals over distances of several
hundred yards. Intriguingly, the canister bombs
were sometimes filled with malodorous but harmless
substances, to trick the enemy into thinking they
were being exposed to harmful gases.

The bodies of hundreds
of Italian soldiers lie dead
on the battlefield, victims
of flame attack

Gallipoli Campaign

With Russia as part of the Entente, along with Britain and France, it was in the Allies' interests to have a sea route from the Mediterranean to Russia. This meant having to secure part of the Ottoman Empire, so that safe passage could be made through the Sea of Marmara to the Black Sea, via the Bosphorus. In order to achieve this, a force was sent to seize the Gallipoli peninsula, so that the Dardanelles strait would be under Allied control. Then, the Allied force would continue eastward to take the city of Constantinople (Istanbul), thereby completing the objective. At least, that was the plan. As it turned out, things went disastrously wrong.

Due to Allied commitments at the Western Front, only a small naval expeditionary force was dispatched to invade the peninsula. The terrain was difficult and led to an initial withdrawal. By the time a larger force arrived, the element of surprise had been wasted and the Turks had amassed a considerable force ready to defend their territory. As a result, the Allies found themselves pinned along the coast with the Turks holding the higher ground inland. Both sides continued feeding in reinforcements, but the frontline remained more-or-less frozen.

British troops of the IX Corps on the beach after landing at Suvla on the Aegean coast of the Gallipoli peninsula in Turkey

Dreadnoughts bombard the heights of Chocolate Hill and Lalu Baba and cover our advance from Suvla Bay, Gallipoli, Turkey

After nine months of ferocious hostilities, the Allies finally decided to cut their losses in December 1915, and withdraw. They had lost over 70,000 men, while the Turks had lost about 60,000. It was one of the most costly campaigns of World War I and achieved nothing except to highlight just how wasteful modern warfare could be. Over 11,000 of the Allied losses were ANZAC (Australian and New Zealand Army Corp). They had travelled half way around the world, only to be slaughtered.

Weather conditions on the Gallipoli peninsula made life particularly difficult for the Allies. In the summer it grew unbearably hot, so that corpses decomposed very rapidly and the smell of putrefying flesh filled the air. In the winter it grew unbearably cold, with flash floods filling trenches and drowning troops. The general lack of hygiene also resulted in outbreaks of dysentery. With no prospect of a successful outcome to the campaign, morale fell so low that evacuation was the only option left available.

Turkish troops on parade at Gallipoli, 1915

The Battle of the Somme

The Somme is a river in north-eastern France, just south of Flanders in Belgium. The word 'somme' is derived from the Celtic for tranquillity, which is about as ironic as anything can possibly be. Ironic, because in terms of human loss of life, the Battle of the Somme was one of the most costly of all time, with over a million killed between 1st July and 18th November 1916. The banks of the Somme were anything but tranquil for those tragic weeks and the battle changed the public perception of war forever, because so many families were affected in such a short space of time.

The original intention behind the offensive that marked the beginning of the Battle of the Somme, was for the Allies to punch a hole through the German frontline and attempt to bring the war to a conclusion. However, the Germans proved to be a formidable enemy and prevented a breach from occurring. The battle then developed into a slanging match of countless attacks and counterattacks, so that fighting became contained within a particular area only a few miles wide and about fifteen miles long.

Canadian troops prepare for the charge over the top at the Battle of the Somme, 1916

Although the Somme frontline moved insufficiently
to justify the vast numbers of casualties, it is now
considered to have been a pivotal battle in World
War I, because attrition to the German army was
considerable and led to a retreat a couple of months
later to the Hindenburg line, some forty miles east.
Whereas the Allies were able to reinforce their forces
following the battle, the Germans were not, so they
had suffered a damaging blow.

The tragedy is that it took so many lives, on both
sides, to achieve the necessary bias in strength for the
Allies to get the upper hand. The same result could
have been achieved by sending the million soldiers
home to their families. But that is where World War
I differed from past conflicts. Traditionally, armies
were more representative of populations rather than
comprising such a high percentage of the populations
themselves. As a consequence, battles were fought
more like games of chess, in a chosen location on a
certain day, to determine the winner. As a result,
relatively few lost their lives to the ritual. Modern
warfare had become an unnecessary cull of those who
were needed to maintain the infrastructure of society
when hostilities ceased.

A German soldier wearing a gas mask
about to hurl a hand-grenade from a
trench during The Battle of the Somme

Roll call of the 1st Battalion, Lancashire
Fusiliers on the afternoon of 1 July 1916,
following their assault on Beaumont
Hamel, Battle of the Somme

War-horses, War-dogs and War-pigeons

Perhaps due to the enormous human cost of World War I, it is often forgotten that many animals died in the conflict too. Of course, large areas of natural habitat were turned to fields of mud and laced with poisonous chemicals, so many wild animals would have perished as a result, but here we consider the domesticated animals used by the armed forces in the war effort.

It is reckoned that about half a million war-horses died in the service of both the Allies and the Central Powers. As tracked vehicles, such as tanks and gun tractors, were only introduced and developed during the war, it meant that horses were still the best way of carrying and pulling equipment over uneven terrain. They were also very effective transportation for personnel, either on horseback, as cavalry, on in troop wagons. Horses therefore played an important role at the Western Front while the front lines were fluid and mobile. When the trench warfare began, horses took a supporting role, working between the supply heads and the back trenches, to ensure that ammunition, foodstuffs and other provisions found their way to those who needed them.

On the Eastern Front, where entrenchment was less frequent, horses continued to play a central role in the military movements of the Russians and the Austro-Hungarians. It should be remembered also, that there were few roads in Eastern Europe, so the horse was a vital mode of transport and traction over rough country.

French Lancers on horseback
follow up a German retreat

French troops with dogs, 1916

British soldiers in the south of England train a carrier pigeon to deliver messages during World War I

Incredibly, about a million war-dogs lost their lives in World War I. They were used to carry messages at the Western Front, and in other frontline zones, where it was too dangerous for humans to risk exposing themselves. Portable radio systems were not yet available, so a physical means of delivering messages was essential. As a result, the dogs were actively targeted by the enemy to prevent the communications from reaching their intended destinations. Messages would be inserted in canisters secured to the dogs' collars.

For long-distance communications, thousands of war-pigeons were used.

Having been kept in pigeon lofts at headquarters, they would use their homing instincts to return to those lofts when released in the field. Messages would be inserted into tubes attached to the pigeons' legs. As pigeons are quite swift flyers they stood a reasonable chance of returning without being shot from the skies. Many British homing pigeons flew from Belgium and France to England. It became illegal to shoot pigeons for sport or food, in case they happened to be winged messengers. Also, many peregrine falcons were shot to prevent them from hunting the pigeons en route.

Hindenburg Line

K nown at the time as the Siegfried Line, but now known as the Hindenburg Line, to avoid confusion with a similar boundary in World War II, it was a fortified line of retreat prepared by the Germans as a precautionary measure, just in case they found themselves in a situation where they needed to lick their wounds. As it turned out, the Battle of the Somme depleted the Germans so much that they had no choice but to give up a forty mile swathe of territory in order to fall back.

The Hindenburg Line was a string of fortifications and tank barriers, designed to keep the Allies at bay while the Germans regrouped and replenished their forces. The Germans had a shortage of manpower because they were fighting on two fronts and this is what compromised them into retreat. Added to this, they had problems with the supply of equipment and munitions. Many soldiers with engineering skills were returned to the German industrial regions in an effort to improve production. In the meantime, the remaining German army had to defend the Hindenburg Line until the situation improved.

A section of a Hindenburg trench near Cologne Farm

British and French troops in reserve lines at Le Verquier, 25 April 1917, following the German retreat to the Hindenburg Line.

Wounded Canadian soldiers within the Hindenburg Line are being taken back from the firing lines by captured German prisoners

The British had, themselves, experienced as shortage of shells known as the Shell Crisis in 1915, which resulted in political reforms to ensure that the entire British economy was geared towards the war effort. New factories were built and labour forces recruited to manufacture adequate numbers of shells and the materials needed.

Eventually the fortunes of the Germans seemed to be improving, when Eastern Front hostilities died away due to civil unrest within Russia. The Communists took control in 1917 and it wasn't in their interests to continue fighting the war, because they had their own civil war to deal with. This meant that the Central Powers found themselves able to redeploy redundant forces along the Western Front and once again push westward away from the Hindenburg Line.

However, the Germans had provoked the USA into declaring war by this juncture and US troops had begun pouring into Europe, ready to join the war effort. As a result, the Germans simply could not muster sufficient resources to counter the influx of Allied support. The writing was on the wall for the Germans and the Hindenburg Line came to represent their Achilles' heel during the interwar years. That is why crossing the Hindenburg Line became so symbolic for Adolf Hitler during his invasion of Western Europe in 1940.

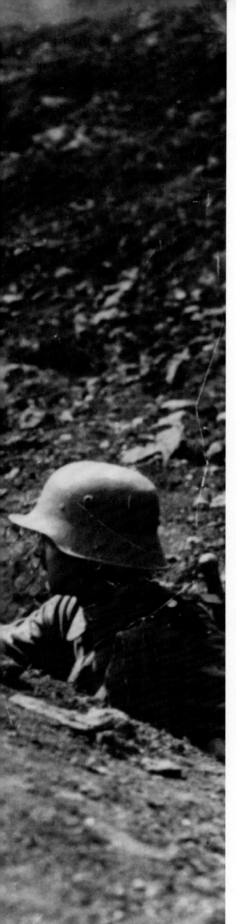
German troops arranging barbed wire defenses to their trench, 1916

Frontline Defenses

As the Western Front descended into trench warfare, it became necessary to put up defenses as protection from enemy fire and from enemy encroachment. The trenches were a form of defense in themselves, of course, as they provided places for soldiers to conceal themselves. In addition, the spoil dug out to form the trenches was used to create bunds in front of the trenches. These would absorb enemy fire and provide additional height for the protection of soldiers.

No-man's-land, the zone between opposed trenches, was another matter. It was desirable to install barricades to prevent the enemy from launching raids, but it was also necessary to be able to see what was going on. This is where barbed wire came into its own. Coils of barbed wire presented a formidable obstacle to would-be raiders, yet it was easy to see through and it had the added advantage of being virtually impossible to breach with grenades and machine gun fire. It was also lightweight and inexpensive.

Many allies and enemy found themselves entangled on barbed wire, which more-often-than-not, meant death from gunfire. It was possible to pass under or through it, but not in a hurry. In fact, the more soldiers struggled the more entwined they became and the more hopeless their prospects became too.

Allied soldier as he stands with fixed bayonet across No-man's-land amid barbed wire obstacles during a battle on the Western Front

When the tank was introduced, however, barbed wire immediately had its limitations. Tanks would roll straight over it and allow pursuing combatants to run across unhindered. Thus the tank changed the rules, so that barbed wire became largely redundant, except in places where tanks could not manage the terrain.

A device called a Bangalore torpedo was invented for the purpose of breaching barbed wire obstacles. It comprised a number of articulated tubes so that, when explosively fired, it would unravel and sweep the barbed wire away. Of course, wire cutters were also available but there was a high risk of being shot whilst attempting to sever the wires. Also, the Germans introduced an extra thick wire, which proved impossible to cut by hand.

The combination of barbed wire and machine guns maintained the stalemate on the Western Front for a considerable period of time. Neither side was able to mobilize for exactly the same reasons, so the war became a process of attrition. Hundreds of thousands died on an un-altering stage, because the theatre of war was unable to travel.

German sniper, lying on the ground behind barbed wire entanglements, 1918

Balloons

When the Western Front had settled into trench warfare, the most immediate problem was acquiring intelligence about what the enemy was up to. For the Germans, this wasn't such a problem, because they had established their positions on what little high ground there was available. These hills were not large, but they gave the Germans a considerable advantage when all around was so flat, as they could observe the Allies.

Aeroplanes were used to make reconnaissance flyovers, but there was always the risk of having them shot from the air and they were expensive to keep in the air for long periods of time. For this reason, balloons were developed by the Allies and the Germans, to enable prolonged observation of activities across no-man's-land.

These observation balloons were filled with either hydrogen or coal gas (a gas mixture) to make them lighter than air. They had to be tethered to the ground by ropes or cables to prevent them from blowing away with the wind, so they were kept well behind the frontline, out of the range of enemy fire. Observers were suspended from baskets below the balloons and communicated with the ground via telephone lines, which hung down.

A German observation balloon is filled with gas, 1915

The launch of a hot-air
balloon used for reconnaissance, 1915

A number of balloon designs were developed
to provide stability for the observers, so that
they weren't forever spinning and changing
direction. The Allies favoured the kite balloon,
while the Germans favoured the drachen
(dragon) balloon. Both had a front end and
a tail, so that they would sit still with the
prevailing wind and allow the observers to
do their job. In order to keep them taut on
their guy-wires, the balloons were fitted with
pockets to catch the breeze, in a similar way to
the sails on a yacht.

On a good day, with sufficient altitude and
clear conditions, observers could see usefully
for twenty or thirty miles, which was especially
useful for instructing artillery batteries in
adjusting their howitzers and field guns.

Due to the risk of being hit by artillery
shells, the balloon operators were the first to
make routine use of parachutes. The packed
parachute had not been invented, so aeroplane
crews had no means of escape, but observation
balloons had hung parachutes, ready for
immediate use.

Barrage balloons were also devised during
World War I, but they were not used in theatres
of battle. Instead, they were used in cities
in an effort to prevent aircraft from making
bombing raids. They were unmanned balloons
that carried cables to deter aircraft, but they
were only effective at relatively low altitudes,
because the cables were heavy to lift.

Austrian soldiers in Albania,
filling a balloon with gas

Trench Design

In typical warfare, trenches are temporary structures, occupied for a few hours or a few days at most. On the Western Front, the situation was entirely different, as trenches were occupied for weeks, months or even years. As a result, their design was rather more considered, from a number of viewpoints. From an offensive point of view, trenches needed to provide soldiers with places to fire weapons and points where it was possible to leave the front of the trench to mount assaults across no-man's-land. From a defensive point of view, trenches needed to protect soldiers from enemy gun and shell fire, and make it difficult for raiding parties to mount effective attacks.

Long-term trenches also needed to be stable, to ensure that the sides didn't collapse. They also needed to include billets, where soldiers could eat and sleep when off-duty. In addition, there was the matter of ablutions and sanitation. In other words, trenches needed to cater for day-to-day requirements of their human occupants over long periods of time.

Trenches were usually equipped with duck-boarding on the ground, to provide an even and dry surface for the soldiers' feet. Wooden shuttering was also used on the sides of trenches to provide stability, and to form the walls and roofs of dug-outs and toilets. Frontline trenches would often include alcoves and bends, so that raiders were unable to simply jump in one end and fire their guns along the entirety of the trench and kill the occupants.

A trench in the low flat country near La Bassee Villa, 1917

An American sniper in France hiding behind barricades, 1918

Many trenches were designed as a system, to allow the rotation of personnel. A central gallery trench, running towards the frontline, would have perpendicular trenches radiating outwards on either side. Typically, there would be frontline trenches, support-line trenches and reserve-line trenches, so that a community of soldiers would take it in turns to carry out different duties. The central gallery trench was heavily defended, because it was the conduit between all other trenches.

All-in-all, life in the trenches was pretty miserable. As well as the constant threat of death, conditions were perpetually dirty and unhygienic, so it was essential that soldiers were given time away from the frontline, to raise their spirits and lift their morale. A number of entertainment troupes were sent to the Western Front for this purpose. They would put on amusing shows to encourage troops to laugh, relax and socialize. Having their minds distracted from the daily horrors of warfare was considered to be vital therapy.

A deserted trench in Ypres, Belgium, site of three World War I battles

Medicine

Disease and infection were responsible for more death in World War I than any other cause. Squalid, unsanitary conditions on the Western Front, the Eastern Front and the Ottoman Front made the likelihood of contracting ailments very high.

Antibiotics had not been discovered, so bacterial infections were a serious problem. Communicable bacterial illnesses, such as tuberculosis, dysentery, typhus and cholera would spread rapidly due to a general lack of hygiene and the close proximity of the combatants. Similarly all battle wounds, large and small, had the potential to become infected, simply because the environment was filled with bacteria. Pieces of rotting cadaver and faeces littered the earth surrounding the trenches. In addition, there were pests, such as rats, flies, fleas and lice, which carried bacteria around with them.

Three German soldiers display rats killed in their trench the previous night, 1916

Many injuries became gangrenous with bacterial infection. The flesh dies (necrosis), leading to blood poising (septicaemia) and then death. Without antibiotics, the only available treatment was to cut the dead tissue away or amputate limbs so that the remaining flesh was free of infection and stood a reasonable chance of healing. Of course, the success of this surgery in turn relied on keeping the newly exposed tissue free from further infection, with the use of disinfectants and dressings. In the field, this was by no means easy to achieve.

Surviving combat injuries was very much a matter of the nature of the injury and its location on the body. Head and body injuries were far more likely to end in death than injuries to the arms and legs. Also, shrapnel injuries tended to be worse than bullet injuries, because the fragments of shell would rip through the flesh, causing considerable damage. Dirty debris would also be introduced to body,

because shells exploded on contact with the ground. Penetrating injuries were always difficult because of the difficulty in removing the foreign bodies and then ensuring that the wound was sterile.

When daily hostilities ceased, stretchers would be used to carry the injured away from the battlefield. The stretcher bearers would be protected from enemy fire by wearing the Red Cross symbol, which was recognized and respected as a sign of benevolence. The injured would then be taken on to field hospitals, which were large tents filled with beds. If there injuries were minor, then they would be treated and send back to the front as soon as possible. If their injuries were more serious, then they would be treated and then sent to proper hospitals farther afield, so that the field hospitals had available beds for new casualties.

A wounded soldier has a bandage wrapped around his face as he receives first aid treatment, 1918

Helping a wounded English soldier on the front in 1915

Officers versus other ranks in a football match played by members of the 26th Divisional Ammunition Train near their camp, just outside the city of Salonika, Christmas Day, 25 December 1915

Keeping Human

Vital to maintaining the sanity of World War I combatants, whether on land, at sea or in the air, were the small things that meant so much. The postal service was an essential part of the war effort as it allowed loved ones to stay in touch by letter when they were parted for long periods of time and there was a good chance they would never meet again. Much of what historians now know about the human side of the war comes from the letters sent during those years. Most surviving soldiers either chose not to discuss the war, or simply were unable too because it was too emotive. The things they had witnessed were best forgotten for the sake of pursuing a happier life, so the way they achieved this was by trying not to think about it. Over time, they put distance between themselves and their memories. Only in old age, did they feel ready to recount their experiences, motivated by their desire to make sure the world did not forget the enormous sacrifice.

In order to while away the time in between periods of action, men would play card and board games. Nearly everyone smoked in those days, so any form of tobacco was highly valued. Regular soldiers were given a two ounce ration of tobacco per week on the Western Front. Other rations included corned or bully beef, bacon, cheese, sugar, tea, jam, bread, biscuits, condiments, vegetables and rum. Germans rations were much the same, although they included cigars, coffee and snuff.

British soldiers eating hot rations in the Ancre Valley
during the Battle of the Somme, October 1916

A female Salvation Army worker writes a letter home for a wounded soldier, 1918

Frontline British soldiers would also receive a basic pay of one shilling per day. This was used to pay for additional items beyond their rations, such as cigarettes, confectionery, beer and spirits when on short-leave. As an indication of how regular soldiers were regarded by the military high command, those working behind the frontline, running supplies and so on, would receive six times as much, even though their jobs were far less dangerous. It seems that the thinking behind this was; that soldiers seldom had a chance to spend their money anyway, so there was no point in giving them very much. Also, there was a good chance that their cash might be lost on the battlefield, so it wouldn't be circulated back into the war coffers. Fundamentally though, regular soldiers were unskilled and working class, so they stood on the bottom rung of the social ladder, despite putting their necks on the line for the nation.

German soldiers cook up a rudimentary meal during World War I, circa 1916

The Early Years

As Winston Churchill and Adolf Hitler were young men during World War I, it is worth considering their involvement to understand how they became the men they were in World War II.

At the outbreak of World War I, Winston Churchill was already a high profile military and political figure. He had been First Lord of the Admiralty since 1911 and introduced a number of important modernizing reforms. However, it was Churchill's idea to mount the disastrous Gallipoli Campaign, so he was forced to resign in 1915. Faced with having to rebuild his reputation, Churchill became an officer at the Western Front, where he took a proactive role and exposed himself to considerable danger. He had exhibited similar reckless daring at the Second Boer War some fifteen years before and it was this fearlessness and determination that would eventually lead the British people to put their faith in him during World War II.

Winston Churchill and General French walk their horses together on manoeuvres during World War I

Adolf Hitler dressed in his field uniform during World War I

Unlike Churchill, Adolf Hitler was yet to make a name for himself when World War I began. He volunteered to serve the German army and became a dispatch runner, seeing action in a number of major battles, including Ypres, the Somme, Arras and Passchendaele. For his bravery and injuries he was awarded the Iron Cross, Second Class in 1914 and First Class in 1918. Having invested so much enthusiasm and effort into the war, he was incensed when the Central Powers capitulated to the Entente and this catalyzed his nationalist ideology that would evolve into Nazism.

Intriguingly, Churchill and Hitler had similarities. They were both attracted to danger as an expression of machismo and both had forged reputations based on those experiences. Also, they both fancied themselves as artists and were competent amateurs at drawing and painting. The difference was that Hitler had wanted to become a professional artist, while to Churchill it was a cathartic pastime.

Both men were certainly egotists, but they came from very different backgrounds and that made them very different as personalities. Churchill came from the British upper class and had a sense of entitlement and expectation, which is why he bent and broke the rules with impunity. Hitler had to climb the social ladder and deal with a fundamental sense of inferiority, which gave him his passion and drive to succeed, but also riddled him with hatred and prejudices. In power, Churchill saw himself honestly, as a flawed leader doing his best for his people. Hitler portrayed himself as a divinely chosen and faultless leader, but underneath he knew the truth, which is why he took his own life when he realized the unlikely game was up.

Corporal Adolf Hitler, right, with two other soldiers and a dog during his stay in a military hospital, WWI, Pasewalk, Pomerania

Trench Raids and Weapons

Due to the loggerhead of trench warfare at the Western Front, soldiers were unable to advance. Day time assaults were suicidal, as the soldiers were cut down by machine gun fire as soon as they went over the top. As a result, night time raids became the modus operandi on both sides.

The objective was to black-up with burnt cork and cross no-man's-land undetected and then enter the enemy trench and dispatch as many of the foe as possible without being heard. This meant that noisy firearms were not to be used, unless their cover was blown and it made no difference. So hand weapons, such as bayonets, trench knives, Bowie knives and knuckle-dusters, were all used and rifles and pistols were kept in reserve.

The principal strategy was to catch sentries by surprise and stab them through the heart or cut their throats, whilst preventing them from shouting out and alerting others. Once the sentries were dealt with, it was then possible to raid billets, simply by lobbing grenades inside and making a quick exit to avoid being caught in the explosion and to escape before reserve soldiers arrived. So, the initial stage of a raid would be silent, but followed by the chaos of explosions and gunfire.

A British soldier in a flooded dug-out in a front line trench near Ploegsteert Wood, Flanders, 1917

Steel helmeted British soldiers in France practice their attack as they hurdle an old trench

With any luck, the raiders would make it back across no-man's-land to live another day, but there was always the risk of being caught on barbed wire or being shot by friendly fire. In an effort to eliminate the possibility of being mistaken for the enemy, raiders used passwords in order to let their own sentries know who they were in the darkness.

Periscopes were often used by sentries to keep an eye on no-man's-land without the risk of being shot. If they suspected a raid might be immanent then flares would be fired to illuminate the sky and expose the raiders, so that machine gunners could see their target and open fire.

This tit-for-tat raiding was an on-going part of trench warfare and was encouraged by high command, because it prevented soldiers from losing their combative edge. The constant risk of being killed and challenge of having to kill, kept the troops psychologically tuned for the job in hand, in readiness for eventual movement in the frontline.

Two British soldiers waiting for the signal to attack at Ginchy, 1916

Italian alpinists defending an attack from a trench dug into the mountain

American troops
advancing on Cantigny,
France, 28th May 1918

The Flying Aces

As World War I progressed, so did mechanization in the air. It wasn't long before fighter aeroplanes were manoeuvrable and reliable enough to partake in aerial dog-fights. The aeroplanes did not yet pose a significant threat to ground operations, except in a reconnaissance role, so pilots were waging a private battle for air superiority, partly motivated by the intelligence threat but also as a matter of pride.

Aeroplanes were conspicuous and they captured the imagination in a way unlike other machines of war.

As a result, they possessed propaganda value and the pilots were regarded as courageous and romantic daredevils. In this rarefied atmosphere, the phenomenon of the flying ace was born and much exploited by the media of the era, on both sides. The flying ace came to personify the war effort from both the Allied and German perspectives, because the public was able to see a face and read a name, which represented all of those fighting at the Front.

A Sopwith Camel, 1917; being small and lightweight, represented the latest in fighter design at the time

SCAN WITH
layar
See page 5
for instructions

American fighter pilot Eddie Rickenbacker, a commanding officer in the US 94th Aero Pursuit Squadron, poses next to his Nieuport 28 N6169 during World War I

115

German flying ace Baron Manfred von Richthofen (The Red Baron) salutes in front
of the officers and staff of Fighting Squadron No. 11 as they stand in formation

German fighter triplane Fokker Dr 1, plane of the
Baron Manfred von Richthofen (The Red Baron)

Probably the most famous of all flying aces
is Manfred von Richthofen, who went by the
sobriquet Red Baron. This was because he flew
a distinctive bright-red Fokker Dr.1 triplane.
He chalked up eighty air combat victories, before
being killed by enemy fire whilst in the air near
the Somme in April 1918. He had a brother, Lothar
von Richthofen, who was also a flying ace, with
forty victories to his name by the end of the war.
Both were handsome and decorated young men,
making them very popular with the Teutonic
public. Other notable German flying aces include
Oswald Boelcke (40 victories) and Max Immelman
(15 victories).

The German approach to keeping tallies of air
combat victories was far more formal than that
of the Allies, which probably said something
about their ordered and serious approach to life in
general. British, French, Italian and US flying aces
were recognized, but they were celebrated more
modestly and their victory tally records are more
vague, as if it were not all that important. What
mattered was that they had five or more kills, as
that was sufficient to demonstrate that they had
prowess at the controls. After all, many pilots
only lasted a few flights before being shot from
the skies or crashing, so anyone who managed
to both stay alive and kill a few Huns was a hero
regardless of tally.

A concentration camp for German prisoners of war in Surrey

Prisoners of War

During the course of World War I, many combatants found themselves captured by the enemy and held in POW (Prisoner Of War) camps. In all, about seven million were incarcerated between 1914 and 1918. As housing and feeding prisoners was an inconvenience and expensive, both in terms of resources and manpower, most prisoners of war were treated with general disdain and kept in squalid conditions with all expenses spared.

European nations had signed the Hague Convention in 1907, which stipulated that prisoners of war were to be treated humanely and that they were prisoners of the government, not the people. This was important, as it made it clear that the government would be held accountable for any inhumane treatment and torture. All of the main participating nations in World War I had signed the convention, except for the Turks, as the Ottoman Empire was part of Asia.

The Germans kept just short of a quarter of a million Allied prisoners in about three-hundred POW camps. Conditions were typically harsh, as the Central Powers could ill-afford to divert much of their war effort to maintaining and guarding the camps. The officers and guards tended to be old or second-rate soldiers, who were not fit for duty at the frontlines. All aspects of prison life made the experience a test of endurance. Food was poor, sanitation was unhygienic, space was limited and so on. This made the environment such that physical and mental illnesses were commonplace.

The prisoners were, however, allowed to send and receive letters from home, which was an important psychological catharsis and gave them something to focus on. The Red Cross provided modest rations, but these were insufficient to sustain health and life, so the prisoners relied on a lifeline of food parcels sent by their loved ones.

Two German prisoners of war imprisoned in a stable after the Champagne offensive

A number of escapes and escape attempts occurred. Although there was the obvious benefit of being freed from prison conditions, many soldiers, especially officers, had a strong sense of duty and wanted to return to active service. Planning escapes also gave them something to think about to alleviate the tedium, and there was the additional satisfaction in knowing that escapes cost the Germans valuable time and effort in searching for them even if they failed to remain liberated.

Prisoners were also used to perform many kinds of work to assist in the war effort against their own people. As the war dragged on, the Central Powers had a drastic shortage of manpower, so the prison labour force became vitally important. Following the ceasefire on the Eastern Front, the Russians POWs were not released, because Germany could not afford to let go of any assistance in the renewed war effort on the Western Front.

A German officer tying up a Russian prisoner of war, 1916

Intelligence and Espionage

A t the frontline in World War I, reconnaissance was the way most intelligence about the enemy was gathered. This was simply using vantage points, observation balloons, aeroplanes and so on to spy on the enemy's movements. This was done covertly if at all possible, so that the enemy was unaware that it had been compromised. But, overt spying was also practiced, when aircraft would fly over and take photographs, for example.

Trench codes were also used at the Western Front, so that important information didn't fall into enemy hands during trench raids. The only problem was, that code books were required to decipher incoming messages and to compose outgoing messages. This meant that code books would need to be very well hidden, or codes would need to be periodically changed. As a result, those at the front were often reluctant to bother with codes even though high command considered it a good idea. It was simply a difference in opinion over the practicality of using codes in real situations , where the perceived advantages could be lost by the time and inconvenience.

A German observer in the basket of
a hot-air balloon using a camera for
aerial reconnaissance

English observation balloon of the Royal Flying Corps

Away from the Front, espionage was rife on both sides, because it was useful to know about the bigger picture, such as major troop movements, supply routes and weapons' manufacture. For this reason, all participating nations had agents whose job it was to gather information and relay it back to those for whom it was useful. This led to double-agents too, who posed as friends but were actually working for the enemy by providing disinformation.

One of the most famous suspected agents was a woman called Mata Hari, a celebrated Dutch burlesque dancer, whose real name was Margaretha Zelle. Being Dutch, she was neutral and able to cross borders during the war, which she did frequently and was consequently questioned by the British counter-espionage team. She was first suspected of working for the French, but then information came to light that implicated her as a German agent. When she went to trial the prosecution could not conclusively prove her guilt, but they stated that she was very likely to be responsible for the deaths of fifty thousand troops. As a result she was executed by firing squad in October 1917, under the rationale that she was probably guilty anyway, and that her publicized death would serve as a sober reminder of the seriousness of furnishing the enemy with intelligence. These days her trial would have collapsed, but the scandal happened at a crucial juncture in the war, when people were getting very weary of the rising death toll and looking for someone to blame.

Reconnaissance in the gorges of the Rajec, An infantry sergeant observing the Prilep road from the Drenovo Pass, Serbia

Admission, Abdication and Armistice

By late September 1918, it dawned upon the German high-command that the war at the Western Front was unwinnable. The hollow victory at the Eastern Front, due to the civil war in Russia, had been used by propagandists to make the German people think that victory at the Western Front was now an inevitable conclusion. In truth, the renewed effort in the west was too little too late. By that time, the Germans were critically short of manpower and resources, and they had provoked the US into joining the Allies. Despite their initial success at moving the frontline by implementing new tactics, they were a spent force and the tide had turned against them.

On the 29th of September, Kaiser Wilhelm II received a communication from General Ludendorff recommending a ceasefire in anticipation that the Allies would soon break through the German lines and take the front eastward to Germany. By 5th October, Germany had asked to negotiate peace with the Allies, but the conditions, including the Kaiser's abdication and withdrawal to the German border, were considered too harsh, so Ludendorff had a change of heart.

By late October, revolution was in the air, as factions of the German military were beginning to turn against the monarchy in favour of a democratic government. As the situation escalated, the Kaiser was forced to abdicate by his own people and the Weimar Republic was announced on the 9th of November. Negotiations with the Allies were concluded at 5 am on the morning of the 11th of November, with the armistice to come into effect at 11am to provide enough time for the word to spread along the Western Front.

SCAN WITH
layar
See page 5
for instructions

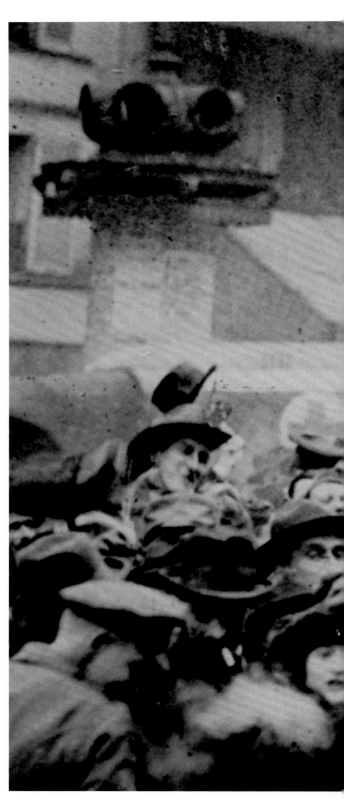

Crowds of people celebrating the signing by Germany of the armistice on November 11, 1918

Newspapers report the abdication of William II, emperor of Germany, November 10, 1918

From the point of view of the German military, the war had come to a premature end due to the political revolution. Largely unaware that the political revolution had actually been a symptom of German attrition, they felt as if they had been prevented from fighting a war they were about to win, so their pride was deeply hurt and they sought people to blame. It was this sense of unfinished business that would prevail in the interwar years and give Adolf Hitler the platform upon which he would build the Nazi cause.

For a while, the new government of Germany was communist, and this is why Hitler was so anti-communist. His subjective view of the armistice made him believe that the communists were to blame for bringing the war to a close and preventing the Germans from having their glorious victory. Had he apprehended that the underlying cause was poor administration of finite German resources, then he might not have allowed history to repeat itself with his own blinkered strategic decisions during World War II.

Excited London citizens cheering in streets and from atop double decker bus after news of the World War I armistice signing is heard

Tyne Cot Cemetery, the largest Commonwealth war grave cemetery in the world, near Ypres, Belgium

The Socio-political Legacy

If we are to find something positive in the wholesale slaughter of World War I, then it is best to consider the revolutions and reforms that it catalyzed in Europe and elsewhere in the world. Above all else, it prompted the rise of the common man in society, simply because so many had made the ultimate sacrifice and so many families were left affected by the war in one way or another.

In Britain, the erosion of the class system had been initiated and voting reforms allowed the masses to have a much greater say in who should be elected to government. Significantly, women over the age of thirty were also allowed to vote for the first time in the post-war election of December 1918. British suffragettes had been actively campaigning before the war, but had agreed to contribute to the war effort in 1915 when it became apparent that the conflict was going to last for some time.

Due to the loss of so many young men, there was also a shortage of manpower in post-war Britain. This marked a social change, because those available to work had a greater say in terms of pay, working conditions and prospects for promotion. In effect, this ushered in the true middle-class, as Britain became a meritocracy, allowing people to climb the social ladder according to their skills and abilities. Prior to that, people very much belonged to the class in which they were born, so relatively few had the opportunity or wherewithal to become upwardly mobile.

Another aspect of the legacy of World War I was the early signs of empire disintegration. Many British colonies had taken part in the conflict and lost considerable numbers of people, yet there was no perceivable gain to be had from it. As a result, the seeds of independence were sown, because those populations realized that they would be better off governing themselves and making their own decisions. The brave new world was just around the corner.

Meanwhile, Russia was undergoing its transformation into a communist nation. The royal family had all been executed and the Bolsheviks had taken control under Lenin. The general Russian population had enough of living in poverty, while the aristocracy lived in luxury. Due to the interrelatedness of the European royal families, the inclusion of Russia in World War I had seemed like a cosying gesture on the part of the Tsar and Russian society was ripe for political revolution.

British POWs being given refreshments on a London railway platform on their arrival back in Britain

The picture shows the revolutionists on the second day of the Russian Revolution

French Prime Minister Georges Clemenceau (left), US President Woodrow Wilson (centre) and British Prime Minister David Lloyd-George (far right) leaving the Palace of Versailles after signing the Treaty of Versailles, Paris, 28th June 1919

The Ember Left Glowing

G eneral John Pershing, who led the American Expeditionary Force in World War I, was very much against the idea of an armistice with Germany. He wanted to defeat the German army in no uncertain terms and warned that the Germans would only rise again if allowed to think that the war ended in a draw. So it was, that an ember was left glowing in the ashes, ready to be fanned back into flames.

The terms agreed for the armistice, which was officially signed at the Treaty of Versailles on 28th June 1919, were quite harsh on the Germans, to ensure that they were rendered unable to launch any new offensives. The result was economic collapse in post-war Germany and this only served to nurture resentment towards the Allied powers.

By 1920 the Nationalist Socialist Workers' (Nazi) Party had been established in Germany to counter the communist movement, held to account for the state of the nation at that time. Adolf Hitler became leader of the party in 1921 and happened to possess a gift for public speaking that captured the imaginations of many disillusioned Germans, who were seduced by the idea of Germany rising once again.

German dictator Adolf Hitler on board a ferry in the Baltic Sea, 1921

Hitler saluting at a Nuremberg rally, 1934

In addition, Hitler had developed resentment for Jews, because they seemed to be well of in relation to the rest of the population, but kept their wealth to themselves and were disinclined to show benevolence. Thus, Hitler had his targets for vilification, which he would use to whip up a frenzy of hatred and blame. Communists and Jews were to be the pariahs of the German nation, enabling Hitler to provide his followers with a collective focus for their frustrations, which actually had nothing to do with the truth but served as a very effective political tool.

In order to give the Germans a sense of behavioural cohesion, the Nazis also introduced notions of Aryan purity and perfection by educating the young with quasi-Darwinian ideas. This led to the additional persecution of anyone who didn't fit with the ideal. The physically disabled, the mentally ill and those from other races and religions were all on the list of undesirables.

Between 1918 and 1939, Germany had lifted itself from its knees and resolved to restore its own pride by once again attempting to conquer Europe. Pershing's prophecy had come true, only this time it came with a far more dangerous ideology that brainwashed the German army into believing it belonged to the master race. In the end though, it would be that delusion of superiority that would lead to the fall of the Third Reich.

Adolf Hitler addresses soldiers with his back facing the camera at a Nazi rally in Dortmund, Germany, 1933

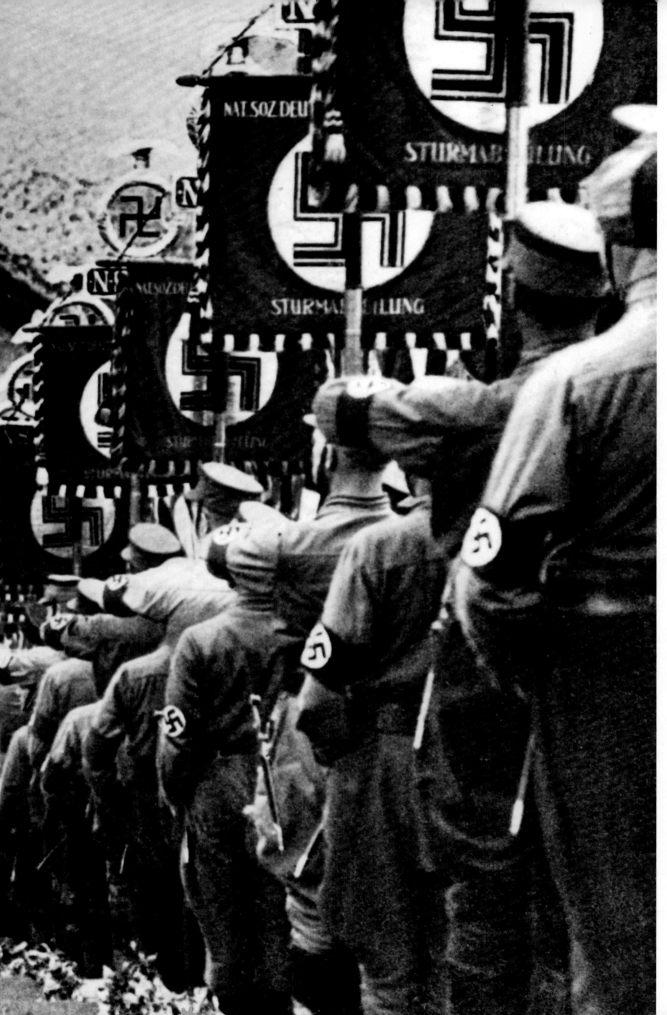

Adolf Hitler walks up
swastika-lined steps with
other party functionaries
during a mass rally,
Germany, 1934

137

WORLD WAR TWO

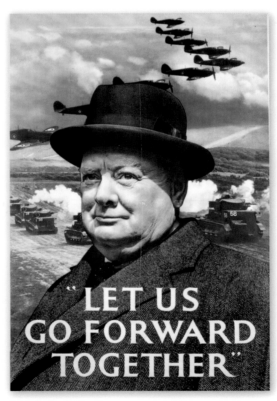

Let Us Go Forward Together
(Churchill) an iconic WWII poster

A news boy selling the News
Of The World carries a poster
proclaiming Britain's declaration
of war on Germany, 1939

An American soldier from 7th
Armored Division mans the
machine gun of his tank while
on manoeuvres, 1942

Troops from the 48th Royal Marines at Saint-Aubin-sur-mer on Juno Beach, Normandy, France, during the D-Day landings, 6th June 1944

Bellicose Bullies

Had Germany and Japan historically invested more time and effort into empire building over the eighteenth and nineteenth centuries, then they wouldn't have been in positions where they had territorial designs on neighbouring nations for the sake of gaining resources. Instead of negotiating access to worldwide resources the subtle way, over centuries, by colonizing second and third world populations, they found themselves wanting because they had been too insular. So, lacking the skills of diplomacy that are learnt and honed by experience of long-term empire administration, both Germany and Japan decided to go about it the aggressive way. Like the playground bully, instead of earning their pocket money by negotiating Saturday jobs, they opted to steal it from those who had earned it. As we all know, bullies may succeed initially by pushing around and intimidating, but sooner or later the victims rally support and pin the bullies against the wall.

Prior to the early twentieth century, Japan had been very inward looking. Culturally, the Japanese had developed a suspicion of the outside world because they were an island nation and felt vulnerable to invasion and conquest. If we draw a parallel with the British Isles, it is interesting to note that invasion and conquest is exactly what made the British so different from the Japanese. British horizons were widened by the flux resulting from the overlay of new peoples, which is why the British were so good at empire building. Opportunism combined with ambiguous cultural identity allowed the British to ambitiously exploit resources across the globe. Meanwhile, the Japanese grew evermore culturally blinkered and disinclined towards international enterprize. By the time they realized the shortcomings of their mind-set, the global village was a different place.

Crowd acclaiming Matsuoka Yosuke, Japanese Foreign Secretary, during a visit in Berlin, 1939

Flags of the allies Japan, Germany and Italy on the building of Japans leading newspaper 'Tokyo Yomiuri', Japan, December 3rd 1937

The Germans had a similar way of viewing the
world to the Japanese, but for different reasons. Quite
apart from being an island nation, Germany had very
little coastline. Instead, it had borders with a number
of other European populations.

The combination of these factors had resulted in
limited empirical ambition compared with other
European nations with relatively long coastlines
and fewer border to defend, such as Britain, France,
Spain, Netherlands and Portugal. To make matters
worse, the Germans had already tried to rampage
their way to a larger territory with World War I, only
to suffer defeat by spreading themselves so thin when
the Allies had inexhaustible colonial resources at
hand. But Germany's resentment at being put in its
place, by peoples it wanted to believe were inferior,
had only given it the resolve to try again and be king
of the castle. As we know though, sand castles are
made of sand and they collapse when their footings
are steadily eroded away.

Adolf Hitler arrives at a military
parade for the celebration of his
50th birthday on April 20, 1939

The Axis

The term 'Axis' was used by the Allies to describe the enemy nations in World War II because Germany, Austria and Italy formed a central line of axis running north to south, dividing Europe in two. The term remained in use when Japan allied with Germany as a matter of convenience.

What Germany and Japan had in common was their delusion of superiority towards other races which, as any psychologist will tell you, is actually an expression of insecurity and inferiority, for those who possess equanimity do not harbour such ideas. In the case of Germany, the primary targets of prejudice were Jews and other peoples who were not Aryan. They also had disdain for any societies, cultures and politics that clashed with Nazi ideals and nations that were not Teutonic. In addition, they had quasi-Darwinian notions about racial purity and perfection, which prompted them to purge their own population of individuals with physical and mental disabilities.

Vidkun Quisling, Norwegian fascist politician who collaborated with the Axis powers during World War Two

The Japanese cultivated particular hatred for the Chinese, because they were the traditional enemy across the sea. Their culture included unquestioning reverence for their emperor, whom they believed was a living god, and this allowed them to believe that they were a divine race. In turn, this gave the Japanese a quasi-Darwinian understanding of strength, which meant that most were prepared to fight to the death as a matter of honour. This furnished them with a marked disdain for enemy forces that were prepared to surrender, rather than fight to the end.

As both Germany and Japan had very clear delusions of racial supremacy, they would have loathed one another had they not had political reason to become allies. It was in both of their interests to ally because their geographical separation meant that enemy forces would need to be divided, to effectively fight two wars. This was an attractive proposition, as both were well aware that the Central Powers of World War I had ultimately lost the war due to attrition of finite resources against an enemy able to source further resources. The fundamental strategy, common to both Germany and Japan, was to capture new resources and utilize them along the way, thereby preventing attrition from becoming a determining factor and allowing both nations to permanently secure new territories.

German chancellor Adolf Hitler (left) and Italian dictator Benito Mussolini in jovial mood during a drive through the streets of Florence, Italy, 1938

A meeting of leaders of the Axis powers in Germany (front row, left to right) Hermann Goering, Benito Mussolini, Adolf Hitler and Count Galeazzo Ciano, 1932

Bewildered investors mill about at Wall Street, New York, after
the Stock Market collapse on 'Black Friday, October 1929

The Great Depression

In October 1929, the Wall Street Crash occurred in the USA, marking the beginning of the Great Depression. Germany had been loaned large sums of money by the Americans following World War I, due to the cost of having to rebuild its economy. After the Wall Street Crash, the Americans had no choice but to call in the monies owed to it and gave Germany ninety days to begin repaying. The knock-on effect of this was to cause amplified inflation in Germany. The value of money dropped so rapidly that it wasn't worth the paper it was printed on and the German population suffered extreme hardship as a result.

At the time, Adolf Hitler was already leader of the Nazi party in Germany and he used the Depression to his advantage by whipping the nation into a frenzied desire for social reform. He was in the right place at the right time, as it didn't take much to sell the idea of a Germany reborn as a European power to be reckoned with. Having captured his people's imagination, the foundations were laid for Hitler's rise to power. The establishment disliked Hitler and did their level best to prevent Germany from falling under his spell, but by 1933 the nation was on the verge of civil war, such was the divide in opinion about how to stage the German recovery. On January 30th Hitler became Chancellor, much to Hindenburg's indignation, who famously called him "the little corporal" alluding to the true nature of his personality. Under Hitler's leadership the nation then rallied to deliver the promise of renewed German might.

The Berlin Stock Exchange remains shut as a result of the closing of the London Exchange during the Great Depression in the United Kingdom, Monday 21st September 1931

Japanese troops marching through Shanghai, 1937

For Japan, the Great Depression had a different though no less significant impact. The Japanese economy had been very reliant on the trade of luxury goods in exchange for natural resources, which it lacked. When the financial slump impacted the world, Japan suddenly found that other nations drew back their purse strings. Japan's export trade fell by fifty percent and things looked bleak. Soon afterwards, in 1931, Japan invaded Manchurian China, to access resources and provision itself with territory in which to build and house its expanding population. A military dictatorship came to power, with Emperor Hirohito as its figurehead, and the stage was set for the further expansion of the new Japanese Empire that was to follow.

Both Germany and Japan responded to the Great Depression by nurturing and then implementing designs on neighbouring territories to access the resources they needed. They saw it as a necessary means to an end, while other nations begged to differ and so the world went to war for the second time.

An American aircraft continues on its flight after dropping ammunition by parachutes to waiting Chinese in their fight against the Japanese

The Build-up to War

In the years preceding World War II it was evident that Germany had military ambitions, simply because of the rhetoric used by Adolf Hitler. There was also a considerable increase in the manufacture of arms and machines of war, as well as the active recruitment of young men into the Nazi Party and German forces. However, politicians in other European countries had the naïve idea that avoiding conflict was a matter diplomacy. They invested a great deal of time and effort into visiting Hitler, thinking that he would be swayed by their good will. In fact, they were making the mistake of judging him by their own standards, for the truth was that Hitler had every intention of putting his plans of conquest into action regardless of these gestures. He was merely pulling the wool over their eyes as he prepared for all-out warfare. When the time was right, Hitler simply got on with what he had always intended, confident that nothing and no one could stop him.

A similar situation had arisen in Japan. There too, military resources were being amassed to set the wheels of territorial ambition in motion. With the Japanese emperor on the throne, the regime itself didn't need a particular personality to take the lead, but the intent was clear. As the Japanese already had a foothold in Manchuria, they had a pre-prepared platform from which to launch their campaign.

German propaganda poster from 1934 reads
'Help Hitler Build – Buy German Products'

Nazi party members listening to a speech by Hitler, 1930

Germany's first move was to annex an area of territory in 1938, known a Sudetenland, which was home to German speaking populations in Czechoslovakia. Then, in 1939, the Germans prepared to invade Poland for the purpose of expanding the German living space. The British warned Germany that war would be declared if the Germans set foot in Poland, so Hitler duly instructed his army to encroach Polish territory on September 1st. Britain declared war on Germany two days later on September 3rd. As the Germans moved into Poland from the west, the Russians invaded Poland from the east as a counter measure, fearful of Hitler's underlying ambitions.

The Japanese began the second phase of their invasion of China in 1937 by capturing Beijing. They then progressively took further swathes of territory. This was known as the Second Sino-Japanese War, and Japan did not enter World War II until 1940 when it joined the Axis, having invaded the colony of French Indo-China, which is now known as Vietnam.

German troops remove the border barrier between Poland and Germany during the invasion of Poland, 1939

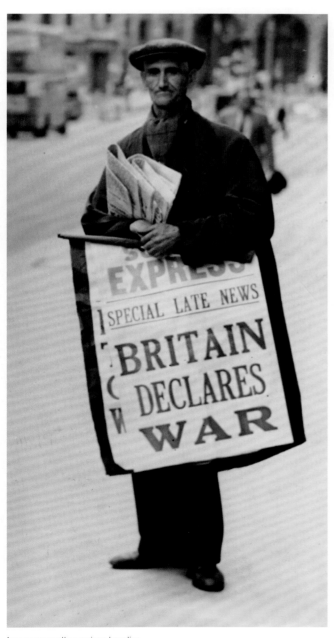

A newspaper seller carries a hoarding
pronouncing the declaration of war
between Britain and Germany, 1939

A crowd gathered to listen as Prime
Minister Benito Mussolini declares
war on Britain and France, 1940

SCAN WITH
layar
See page 5
for instructions

157

The Political Map

The political map at the beginning of World War II wasn't greatly different from that of World War I, especially in Europe. This was because Germany was again the main protagonist against the Allies, and the countries that joined the Axis either contained Germanic populations or were so dominated by the Third Reich that they had more to gain by siding with the Germans. In the case of Italy, it was led by the Fascist dictator Benito Mussolini, who was an ardent admirer and follower of Adolf Hitler. Thus the European Axis comprised Germany, Italy, Hungary, Romania and Bulgaria. Austria was part of Germany at that time, and known as Anschluss. The Asian wing of the Axis was solely represented by Japan.

To begin with, the European Allies comprised United Kingdom, France and Poland, but many other nations were drawn in on the Allies' side as the war progressed. Asia was represented by Russia and China, while the New World was represented by USA, Canada, Brazil and Mexico. Australia, New Zealand and South Africa were also with the Allies.

As the war moved into 1940 and then into 1941, the political map evolved as the Axis powers invaded new territories. Some conquered nations resisted occupation, while others dealt with their lot by cooperating, for the sake of survival. Similarly, the political map evolved further when the Allies forced the Axis into retreat. A number of European colonies in Asia and Southeast-Asia had become more autonomous under Japanese occupation and resisted having to return to colonial control when they were liberated.

The flags of Fascist Italy and Nazi Germany flying together, 1937

A member of the French Resistance, taking cover behind truck from a German sniper during fight

Although Russia was on the side of the Allies, it had its own agenda too. While most of the Allies were mainly interested in defeating the Axis and restoring the political map, the Russians saw an opportunity to seize eastern European territories and enlarge their territory, as if Russia wasn't already large enough. The motive behind this was communism. Stalin and his cronies had the vision of a modern world dominated by their particular brand of dictatorial communism, so they wanted the political map to include as much red as possible to counter the blue of democracy and capitalism that they knew would exist following the fall of the Axis.

A few nations were anomalous in their intentions, such as Finland. In effect, it fought its own war, as it battled both the Russians and the Germans. Geographically, Finland was strategically advantageous to invade, providing generous access to the Baltic Sea, but the Finns had no desire to be occupied by either one of the opposed forces.

Motivation

The motives for World War I were largely to do with political ideas of pride and honour amongst the ruling classes. This lent itself, very much, to the overriding feeling that millions had lost their lives pointlessly in the aftermath of the war. Fundamentally, the European nations belonged to a shared ideological mind-set. This is why, for example, it was possible for German and British troops to down their weapons and share Christmas together as they did in 1914. This demonstrated clearly that there was a sense that they were only fighting because they had been told to by their superiors. It also expressed an acceptance of subordination and class hierarchy, because that is all people knew at the time.

World War II was different in this regard, as European class structures had been eroded, so that people were no longer naïve enough to risk death for no real reason. However, people were willing to fight for an ideological cause, and this is what they got. The Nazi regime had conditioned many Germans into believing they were a master race, destined to rule Europe, so Hitler had a devoted army who willingly obeyed his every command. Although this worked in Hitler's favour, by generating cohesion in the German population and making them a formidable force, it also worked against him because the Allies were able to use propaganda to motivate their own peoples against the Germans.

Nuremberg Rally, 1934

British and German troops make a Christmas and New Year truce in the trenches of the Western Front, 1915

The Nazis quickly made a reputation for themselves and brutal, merciless killers because they had been conditioned to think of other populations as inferior. This played into the hands of Allied governments, because they were able to portray Germans as evil. The Germans were 'baddies', while the Allies were the 'goodies'. Needless to say, the Germans didn't think of themselves as evil, but rather that they had an inalienable right to rise to power and put other humans in their place. So, it was this ideological disparity that underpinned and incentivized both the Germans and the Allies.

The Japanese had a similar reputation, as cruel and inhuman in their treatment of other peoples, because they too had the idea that they were a superior race. The notion that large areas of the world might end up being controlled by the Nazi and Nippon regimes was made even more unacceptable by this perception of evil intent among the Allies that an absolute determination arose to defeat the Axis at any cost, for the sake of restoring the world to a place of relative goodwill. It may not ever be a utopia, but it was always going to be better than a dystopia.

A smiling member of the female branch of the Hitler Youth, carrying a collecting tin, circa 1938

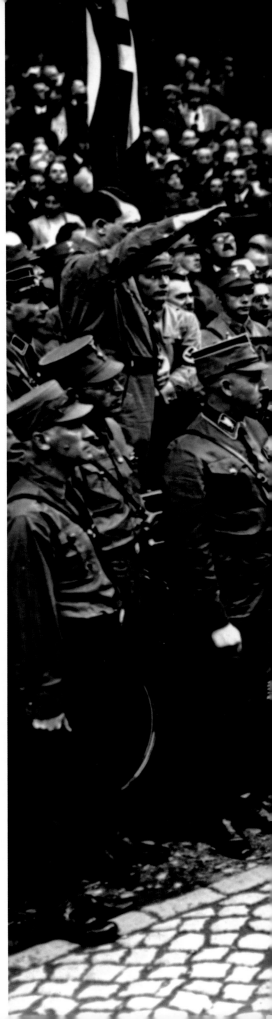

German dictator Adolf Hitler takes the salute at a Nazi parade in Germany

A member of the Hitler Youth with a swastika flag at a Nazi rally in Germany

German troops entering Poland after a 'blitzkrieg'

German soldiers using flamethrowers against a
French bunker on the Maginot Line, 1940

A scene typical of many French towns in northern
France with destruction and chaos everywhere
following Germany's victory in France in 1940

The Blitzkrieg

Following Germany's invasion of Poland,
resulting in the British declaration of war,
there was a fallow period of inaction, now
known as the Phony War, lasting just over eight
months. During this time, Hitler was sizing up
the enemy and allowing their forces to become
complacent with boredom. He made gestures
suggesting that he was hoping they may acquiesce
and allow him to keep Poland, but it transpired
that he was amassing a large military force ready
to invade France and the Lowlands. When the
offensive was implemented it caught the Allied
forces by surprise. The Germans struck so hard and
fast that there was little the opposing forces could
do except retreat and attempt to slow down the
Nazi advance.

The Germans had introduced a new mode of warfare
called Blitzkrieg (Lightning-War). It was designed
to be swift and overwhelming, rather like a tsunami,
so that resistance was futile. A German officer,
named Heinz Guderian had developed the concept in
the early 1930s by optimizing tank design along with
that of armoured cars and artillery, so that they
were highly effective at moving rapidly over rough
terrain. He had also fully equipped the tanks and
military units with radios, so that communication
was state-of-the-art and efficient. As the tanks
forged their way forwards, blasting any key
opposition units out of action, they were followed
by crack divisions of storm troopers, who dealt with
the enemy troops while they were still in a state of
disarray. To the rear, artillery would be instructed
to take out any enemy positions inaccessible to
the tanks.

The spearhead of the Blitzkrieg emerged from the Ardennes forest on the 10th May, 1940 and proved unstoppable as it widened and continued westward. Another advantage of its rapid progress was that the Allies were unable to relocate and deploy forces from elsewhere to impede the Blitzkrieg. Added to that, the Allies' equipment was inferior and they had a different strategic mind-set, so they were outgunned and outmanoeuvred. To avoid being killed or being taken captive, the Allies had no choice but to make a rapid tactical retreat and figure out what to do next.

An important factor in the success of the Blitzkrieg was air support. The German air force, the Luftwaffe, was very effective at dive-bombing Allied columns and strategically bombing installations farther afield. This had the effect of weakening supply lines and softening targets to enable the offensive to continue unabated. All in all, the Germans had devised a war machine, which the Allies were unable to counter at that stage of the war, thereby allowing the Germans territorial purchase on mainland Europe.

New Race to the Sea

German soldiers going on the attack on the Western Front in France, 1940

During the opening stages of World War I, the Allies had been successful in preventing the Germans from reaching the coast of France and Belgium. When it came to World War II, the Allies were not so fortunate. When they realized that the German forces could not be stopped it put a whole new complexion on the situation at hand. The British decided that the best plan of action was to use the sea to their advantage and organize a mass evacuation, thereby leaving the Germans on the coast.

The point of evacuation was to be a small French town named Dunkirque (Dunkirk) and the operation, named Dynamo, began on 27th May, just seventeen days after the Blitzkrieg had begun. On the 28th May, the French army began defending the area around Lille to stall the Germans and give the British a chance to get away. They held up for four days before the Germans punched their way through, but it had done the trick. By the 4th of June the evacuation was complete, so that most of the British force had escaped, along with many French soldiers.

The port Dunkirk shrouded in smoke after fires had been started by German bombing

Over nine-hundred vessels had been used to evacuate 198,000 British and 140,000 French troops back to British shores. The majority of the rescue fleet had been non-military boats responding to the crisis and risking shellfire to stow as many soldiers as they could. Some craft made several round trips over the nine days of evacuation, which saved a third of a million combatants from death or incarceration. More importantly, it meant that the Allies still had an intact fighting force, albeit stationed on the wrong side of the English Channel, or la Manche as the French call it.

So, the Germans had won the Battle of France in some style, but that was just one battle with many more to come. A little over four years later, many of those evacuees would return to French shores as part of the Normandy Landings and begin the process of pushing the Germans all the way back to Germany.

The evacuation of Dunkirque has taken its place in British folklore, because it was a classic example of people making the best out of a bad situation. The participation of so many civilians also demonstrated cohesion of spirit against the enemy and gave the British something to be positive about at a time when their future was by no means certain.

The ruins of Dunkirk after the fighting had ceased

Tanks Come of Age

The tank was first conceived by the British during World War I, as a means of crossing the battleground under machinegun fire to break the deadlock of trench warfare. By the close of World War I the French had come up with the design that would become the standard format for tanks as we know them today. The Renault FT had a rotating gun turret mounted on an armoured chassis with the engine positioned at the rear and the driver positioned at the fore. This pattern set the standard that saw tanks evolve into efficient fighting machines during the interwar years.

The Germans developed a series of Panzer tank prototypes over the 1930s. They were considered to be better designed than most of the tanks of the Allies, in terms of reliability, manoeuvrability and weaponry, but it was the Blitzkrieg tactics that made them so much more effective in the field of battle, as it enabled the Germans to avoid one-to-one tank confrontations. The Germans were also the first to fully equip their tank corps with radio communications, which made a vast difference in terms of strategy. The Panzer III and Panzer IV were the models used in the early part of World War II. They were relatively small tanks and by the close of the war the Germans had introduced a medium tank in the form of the Panther and a large tank in the form of the Tiger. The Panther was a particularly effective weapon and set the benchmark for all post-war tanks.

A German Panzer IV, 1941

The Russians prompted the Germans to improve their tanks, because they had a model called the T-34, which proved superior to the Panzers on the Eastern Front. Britain had various Cruiser and Infantry tanks, but also used American General and Sherman tanks. Sherman tanks were cheap to mass produce, which is what the USA did best, so there were plenty available even though they lacked sophistication and quality. Two or three Sherman tanks against a Panzer were always going to win, even though inferior in design. In the end this was a critical factor against the Germans, as they lacked the resources to manufacture enough of their tanks, partly because their quality standards were too high.

The Japanese had well designed tanks too, but they were not frequently used due to geography. In fact, they kept many of their tanks in reserve in case they had to defend their homelands, so they were never used. The Chi models of tank were the most advanced of the Japanese designs.

Turret crew of a 1st Royal Tank Regiment A9
Cruiser Mk I tank at Abbasia, Egypt

A US M4 Sherman tank

Panzer units of the
German Army pass
through a blazing
Russian village

Aeroplanes Come of Age

The aeroplane was still in its infancy during the years of World War I, it began life as a reconnaissance vehicle, but its potential as a weapon was becoming evident as more reliable and faster models were being produced. By the close of the war, the aeroplane was beginning to evolve into particular classes of aircraft too, so that the concept of fighters and bombers had emerged.

During the interwar years the aeroplane continued to evolve rapidly. As engines developed to become more powerful relative to size, this meant that faster, stronger and heavier aeroplanes could be engineered.. The aeroplane was no longer a flimsy, slow moving target, but a sleek, fast-moving war machine.

With increased speed, most aeroplanes became monoplanes to optimize their performance and manoeuvrability, and most adopted the standard format of fuselage with two flight wings to the fore and tail-plane to the rear. Other designs were all variations on the same theme even though they could be quite varied in detail.

Henschel HS 123 Dive Bomber, This single-seat biplane with swastika was originally used by the German Luftwaffe during the Spanish Civil War

Japanese seaplane wrecked during the battle of Makin, November 1943

The wreckage of a
German Heinkel bomber
which crashed on the
north-east coast of Britain
after an encounter with
RAF fighters

Aeroplanes Come of Age | **World at War**

German machine gunner in a military aircraft, 1939

Bombers needed to have large wing areas and a
number of engines to provide sufficient payload,
not just for bombs, but also for the fuel necessary
for long-distance missions and the crews need to fly,
navigate and defend the aircraft. Fighters needed to
be single-engined with relatively low wing area to
make them fast and acrobatic in the air. They needed
to carry sufficient fuel to escort bombers, but they
had only a single pilot and machineguns as
additional payload.

There were intermediate aeroplanes too, in the form
of fighter-bombers, which were somewhere between
the two in terms of size, speed and payload. They
were designed for medium range missions, where they
could fly alone and make more precise bombing raids
at low altitude. The Germans developed a fourth types
of combat aeroplane, known as the dive-bomber.
The idea was that the aircraft would dive towards
its target and jettison its bombs forwards before
levelling off. That way, it could hit the target with
deadly precision.

A range of support aircraft were also developed
for various purposes. There were cargo planes to
transport supplies, equipment and personnel. There
were also light aircraft for reconnaissance work and
for covert field operations. A number of seaplanes
were also developed to utilize flat-water for landing
and taking off where runways were unavailable.
Many fighters were also adapted for use on aircraft
carriers, which were basically mobile runways and
fuelling depots.

A squadron of German Messerschmitt 110
fighter-bombers flies in formation

The Battle of Britain

Having conquered France and driven the British expeditionary force back across the English Channel, Hitler had designs on invading the British Isles, which he called Operation Sea Lion. In order to prepare for the planned invasion he knew that it was essential to first take on the RAF, so that the British would lack the air support necessary to defend their coastline against the offensive. So, the Luftwaffe was tasked with the job of destroying the British air force. The ensuing war for air superiority became known as the Battle of Britain.

As the Battle of Britain was primarily fought in the air, it meant that fighters were the key aircraft. The British had the Hurricane and the Spitfire at their disposal, while the Germans had the Messerschmitt Me109 and the twin-engined Messerschmitt Me110. In terms of hierarchy, relating to all-round performance, the Spitfire came first, followed by the Me109, then the Hurricane and the Me110. This gave the British the technical advantage, but they had fewer aircraft, so the odds were about even. Britain had just short of two thousand aeroplanes, while Germany had just over two and a half thousand.

Strategy, tactics and intelligence were therefore central to tipping the odds in favour of the British. Hugh Dowding had the position of Fighter Command at the start of the battle, on 10th July, 1940. He implemented very efficient ways of utilizing the resources available to him. In particular, he had small squadrons scattered across the country and an advanced radar system, which allowed pilots to be scrambled at a moment notice to intercept enemy aircraft. By a process of attrition, the Luftwaffe was systematically depleted of its aircraft, until the battle was declared won by the British on the 31st October, 1940.

A Spitfire I, one of the first to be supplied to the RAF

Hawker 'Hurricane' planes from no.111 squadron

The British Prime Minister, Winston Churchill, was moved to say "Never before, in the field of human conflict, was so much owed, by so many, to so few." In winning the Battle of Britain, the RAF had caused Hitler to postpone Operation Sea Lion until the following year. By then, his concerns lay at the Eastern Front and Britain was left to lay its plans for an eventual counter offensive. In anticipation of a possible invasion, Churchill had also said "We shall fight on the beaches, we shall fight on the landing grounds, we shall fight in the fields and in the streets, we shall fight in the hills; we shall never surrender," but as it turned out the Battle of Britain had prevented that eventuality.

SCAN WITH
layar
See page 5
for instructions

Domestic War Effort

Fundamental to all successful war campaigns is logistics-organizing the manufacture of resources and the administration of their supply to where they are needed. When Britain realized that World War II was going to take a long time and rely heavily on effective logistical management, the government had to make some vital decisions and issue directives to the general population in order to involve the entire nation with the war effort.

Rationing was an important part of this objective as it meant that people were only too aware of the need to value and conserve basic resources, such as foodstuffs and domestic substances, such as washing powder and soap. This was partly because the forces needed to be supplied with basic necessities overseas, but it was also because many goods were imported and vessels were put to better use carrying cargoes of war equipment and munitions. In addition, German submarines were doing a very good job at preventing cargo ships from reaching the British Isles. As a way of supplementing their diets, the British people were encouraged to grow vegetables and rear livestock on any available plot of land, and to make the most of seasonal harvests of fruits and nuts.

Volunteer American pilots during the Battle of Britain

A close-up of a British ration book

Women working in a munitions factory, 1943

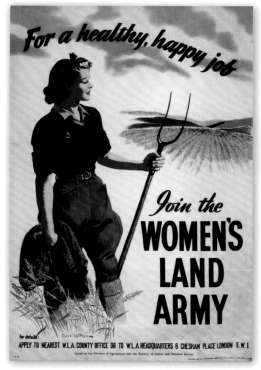

Recruitment poster for the
Women's Land Army

Members of the Women's Land Army gather the late harvest on a farm in Llangwm, Wales

Another area, where the general population were asked to assist, was in the provision of war materials-particularly iron and aluminium. Iron was used for making armour plating, gun barrels and other engineering components, such as nuts, bolts, rivets, and cogwheels. Aluminium was used in the manufacture of aircraft, because it was lightweight. Other metals included lead, for bullets, and copper and brass for shell casings.

Civilians were also asked to contribute their time and effort into war related duties, such as the manufacture of machines and weapons. Many women volunteered to work in factories, so that they could play their part in the war effort while their husbands, brothers and fathers were away.

Their children had often been evacuated to live in rural locations where they were less likely to be bombed.

Many young women helped the war effort by leaving towns and cities to work on farms as 'land girls'. As most farm labourers had been enlisted into the army, air force and navy, the replacement workforce was extremely valuable in ensuring that British farms kept up production of cereals, vegetables, meats, eggs and dairy produce. The land girls were largely responsible for providing the nation with the rations it needed to survive the war.

Two Wehrmacht soldiers are holding a Swastika flag to protect against friendly fire during Operation Barbarossa

Operation Barbarossa

Following the German invasion of Poland in 1939, Hitler had agreed a pact of non-aggression with Russia in August of that year. At the time it suited Hitler to pretend that he had no interest in invading Russia, so that he could concentrate his resources in Western Europe. By the close of 1940 Hitler decided that he only needed an occupying force in the west, so he made plans to break his pact with Russia and head eastward. In the spring of 1941 deployed a huge fighting force along the Eastern Front and launched their offensive, named Operation Barbarossa, on June 22nd.

At first, the German assault was a success, as it had been on the Western Front. The Blitzkrieg tactics worked well and the Germans made rapid territorial gains. Hitler was delighted with progress and had every confidence that Moscow would be taken, so that Russia would become
part of the Third Reich. However, things began to go wrong as winter closed in on the Germans. Muddy ground made it difficult for the frontline to move forward and it made the supply chain inefficient. In addition, the troops were ill-equipped to operate in the wet, cold conditions. When the Russian winter set in properly it was so cold that engines wouldn't start and soldiers were suffering from frostbite. The mighty German army had been halted by the Russian climate.

Russian soldiers in the snow during winter
1941- 1942 on the Russian Front

A soldier is guarding a village under the snow

In addition, the Russian population was so large that Stalin had an almost endless supply of new troops. They died in vast numbers, but were replaced in equally vast numbers, so that attrition was gradually depleting German resources. Being used to their own climate, the Russians were also far better equipped, both physically and mentally, to cope with the conditions.

By December 1941 the Germans were only a matter of miles from Moscow, when Stalin gave the order for the Russian counter-offensive on December 5th. The Germans were unable to defend their positions and were pushed into a momentum of retreat. By mid-December the weather was so cold that the Luftwaffe were unable to assist, because their aeroplanes were rendered inoperative by the sub-zero temperatures. Operation Barbarossa had turned from success to failure as the Germans were pushed ever farther west. Until weather conditions improved in 1942 there was little they could do to try turn matters back in their favour.

SCAN WITH
layar
See page 5
for instructions

The Blitz

About halfway through the Battle of Britain, on September 7th 1940, the Germans began a strategic bombing campaign of British cities. It became known as the Blitz, not to be confused with the Blitzkrieg and would last for over eight months. The initial incentive for the bombing campaign was to strike at factories dedicated to the manufacture of aircraft, munitions and other equipment. Ports were also targeted to disrupt supply lines. However, bombing was not an accurate science in those days, especially under cover of darkness, so the majority of bombs missed their intended targets and randomly hit residential areas, killing many civilians.

Devastated buildings around St Paul's Cathedral, London, after an air raid during the Blitz

Firemen at work on fires, the result of bombs dropped
by the Germans, near St Paul's Cathedral, London

The main cities bombed were London, Birmingham, Bristol, Plymouth, Birmingham, Southampton and Portsmouth. London suffered more bombing raids than the others combined, so sheltering became a matter of routine. In fact there was an average of around one raid every three or four days, so it was better to be safe than sorry. London lost more than a million homes and over forty thousand people lost their lives. Things were so dangerous that children had to be evacuated to live with families in rural locations for the duration. Despite the death and carnage visited on their city, Londoners displayed a behavioural cohesion known as the Blitz spirit, which saw people helping one another to cope with the practical problems and the emotional trauma experienced by so many.

Due to the inaccuracy of bombing, it was a matter of hit or miss as to whether strategic targets received bomb damage. Some raids were successful in halting British progress, but never for sustained periods of time. They also became self-defeating

as the Blitz only prompted the British to mount retaliatory raids over Germany, so that their own wartime industries were disrupted. This tit-for-tat bombing continued as the war protracted, but civilian deaths became an ethical issue. For one thing, the killing of children, women and the elderly seemed entirely unnecessary. From the British point of view, there was also the notion that many of the German civilian population were not followers of the Nazi ideology, and were therefore innocent victims. Following the war, those who commanded and took part in bombing raids were not properly celebrated and recognized for their contribution to the war effort. This was because of an undercurrent of shame that the bombing of civilian areas had become a component of war. It didn't sit well with the idea that war should be conducted in an honourable way.

Londoners sheltering in an Underground station during an air raid

Below; Tommies of the British forces toil in the heat of the midday sun, in the shadow of the Egyptian pyramids

North Africa Campaign

The North Africa Campaign began when the British decided it would be strategically useful to control the Mediterranean Sea, with a view to launching a counter-offensive against the European Axis from the south. At the time, the region was occupied by Italian forces. The Italians were no match for the British and were pushed into retreat, but Hitler responded by deploying German forces under the command of Erwin Rommel and the complexion of the campaign changed very quickly. There was now parity between the Allied and Axis forces, which resulted in a protracted series of battles, causing the frontline to sweep back and forth as offensives and counter-offensives were launched.

The campaign began in June 1940 and would drag out until May of 1943. The Second Battle of El Alamein

(Oct-Nov 1942) is recognized as a seminal moment in World War II, because it was the first time the Allies had achieved a decisive victory against the Axis. Responding to news of the German defeat, Winston Churchill commented in a speech "Now this is not the end. It is not even the beginning of the end. But it is, perhaps, the end of the beginning". He wanted to accentuate the positive outcome, but he also wanted to make it clear that the war was a long way from being won. Following the eventual Allied victory, he commented that the battle had indeed been a turning point in the war as, from that point onwards, the Germans were on the back foot. Momentum had shifted in the Allies' favour.

Below; Two soldiers belonging to the Commonwealth and Allied forces aim at a German soldier surrendering atop his tank 25 October 1942 as a sandstorm clouds the battlefield at El Alamein

British tanks proceeding along the waterfront in
Benghazi as the 8th Army advance in Libya

The first British tank enters Tripoli, Libya with
soldiers and a piper aboard the Valentine tank

Scottish Cameron Highlander
and Indian troops marching past
pyramids, part of Allied defence
preparations against Italian attack

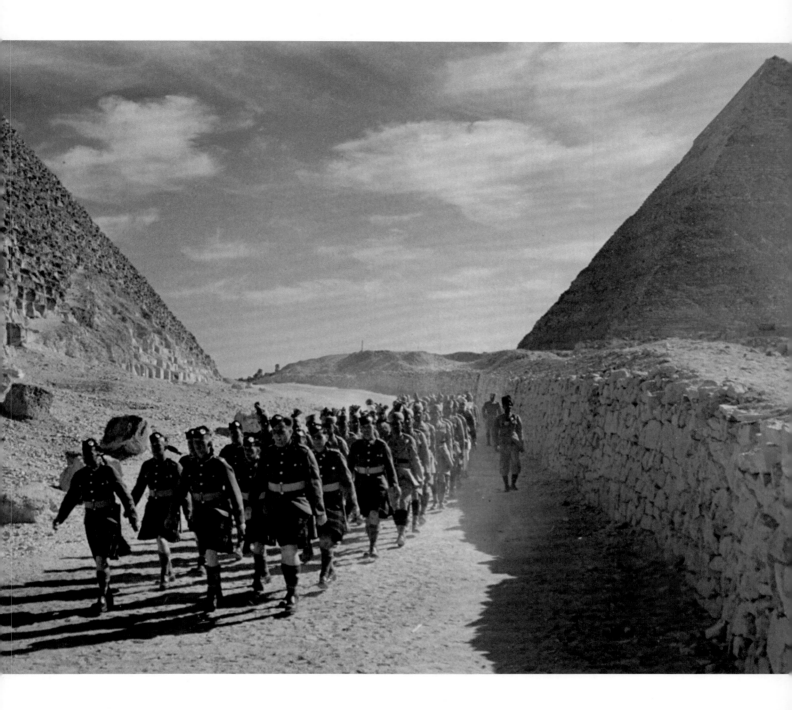

The North Africa Campaign was characterized by the desert terrain, typical of the coastline of the southern Mediterranean. This meant that there was no cover, either from the elements or from enemy fire. Tanks, howitzers and field guns played a central role in the theatre of battle, but the most critical element was one of logistics. As one side advanced, its supply lines became progressively stretched over barren terrain, making it harder and harder to keep the front moving. At the same time, this meant that the supply lines of the opposing force were shortened, making it easier to reach the frontline. As a result, the battle front oscillated west-east/east-west a number of times, until attrition of the German reserves finally allowed the Allies to get the upper hand. The Axis was ultimately forced out of North Africa because sufficient reserves were not made available by Hitler, as he had more pressing concerns elsewhere.

Attack on Pearl Harbor

L ate in 1941, the Japanese had plans to invade the southern reaches of Southeast Asia, including the northern coast of Australia. The indefatigable progress of the Nippon army had the Australians deeply fearful and the Americans were amassing a large fleet in the Pacific, in anticipation of their entry into the war. The Japanese were aware of the US military build-up and decided to force the situation in order to prevent the Americans from halting their empire building.

As the Japanese had not yet declared war on the USA they had a trick up their sleeve-the element of surprise. On the morning of December 7th, they launched an all-out offensive against the US military base at Pearl Harbor, Hawaii. The majority of the US fleet was moored-up in the harbour, so it was like shooting fish in a barrel. The Japanese used over three hundred and fifty aircraft and a number of mini-submarines to wreak havoc on the Americans before they knew what was happening.

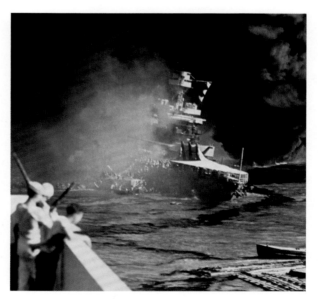

The USS California on fire in Pearl Harbor

USA warships on fire in Pearl Harbor, Oahu Island after a surprise attack by the Japanese

Many important US vessels were destroyed and sunk during the attack, leaving the American fleet seriously depleted. However, the Japanese had failed to destroy many of the essential dock facilities, which meant that recovery was reasonably rapid. Also, both of the US aircraft carriers and their escort convoys happened to be away from port at the time of the attack, so the core of the US fleet remained intact.

In effect, the Japanese had awakened a sleeping giant by attacking Pearl Harbor in the way they did, without declaring war. While the Japanese celebrated what they saw as a cunning victory, the Allies saw the assault as an underhand ambush. In 1937 the Japanese had behaved in a similar way by opening hostilities against China without declaring

war. In repeating this unsporting approach, the Japanese had done themselves no favours as it revealed an underlying disrespect for other nations and fuelling Allied determination to put them in their place.

Once the USA was committed to the war, it wanted revenge for Pearl Harbor, so the Japanese had determined foe on their tail. It took some time for the Americans to replenish their fleet and develop the right strategy for dealing with ensconced Japanese occupying forces, but eventually they were systematically flushing the enemy from one island after the next and forcing the Japanese to constrict their ambitions of empire.

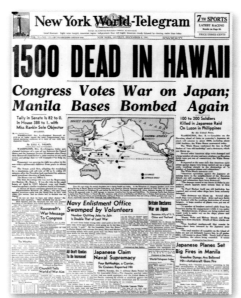

The front page of the 'New York World Telegram'

Troops salvage the wreckage following the attack on Pearl Harbor

Vichy France

Following the Fall of France in the Summer of 1940, the French government felt compromised into reached a peace agreement with Germany in order to save France from being portioned out between the Axis powers. In effect, France became a state of the Third Reich, known as Vichy France. The northern region remained occupied by German forces to defend against possible invasion from across the English Channel, while the southern region was the 'free zone' and maintained its sovereignty.

General Charles de Gaulle had fled to exile in London, from where he rallied support against German occupation of France. He also maintained political opposition towards Marshall Philippe Pétain who had assumed leadership of the regime in collusion with the Germans. Many of those still living in France, who opposed Pétain and the Germans, joined the French resistance movement, named the Maquis. Many of the rest of the population did their best to support and assist the Maquis in their terrorist operations, by hiding weapons and protecting people when they could.

There was also a Europe-wide resistance network to help enemies of the Axis travel through occupied Europe without being captured. This included downed airmen, escaped prisoners, special agents, covert operatives, Jews and fellow resistance personnel.

Algeria, in North Africa, was a French colony when Germany conquered France, so it became part of Vichy France, providing the Axis with control of Algeria in 1940. However, the Vichy army offered only half-hearted resistance against the Allies when they decided to invade Algiers in November 1942, because many were reluctantly fighting for the Axis. As a result, Operation Torch was a success and gave the Allies a solid foothold on the southern Mediterranean coast. This contributed to the British success at El Alamein, because it improved supply lines at a critical juncture.

By chance, the commander in chief of the French Navy, Admiral François Darlan, had travelled to Angiers the day before the invasion and was captured. He turned against the Vichy government by deciding to express allegiance with the Allies. As a result Hitler sent reinforcements to North Africa and ordered the occupation of Vichy France by German and Italian troops to protect the Mediterranean coast of France. However, in North Africa the tables were already turning in favor of the Allies, whose next move would be to make preparations for invading Italy.

Henri Philippe Petain (left), French general and later Chief of State of Vichy France

American troops wade ashore near Oran, Algeria, during Operation Torch, November 1942

Hitler salute At Vichy In France

War in the Atlantic

As World War II progressed, Britain and its allies relied ever more heavily on goods and equipment being shipped from the Americas across the Atlantic Ocean. As a result, the Atlantic became a hunting ground for German submarines, which were known as U-boats. As any large vessels were quite likely to be carrying goods essential for the Allied war effort, in one way or another, the U-boats targeted indiscriminately with their torpedoes. This meant that ships were theoretically safer travelling in convoy, with armed escorts. However, it was double-edged sword, as groups of ships made much easier targets for the U-boats. They were more likely to make a hit and they also had the chance to sink a number of boats in a single raid.

The U-boats also found easy pickings along the American coast. As the Americans were not initially involved directly in the war, they had a rather naïve understanding of the U-boat threat. In particular, they made no effort to blackout their cities, which meant that cargo vessels were nicely silhouetted against the lights at night, making them extremely easy targets for the submarines. They just had to sit in wait and fire torpedoes at will.

German sailors crouch down by the U-boat's conning tower as they manoeuvre against an attack by American B-25 Mitchell and B-24 Liberator bombers, 1944

However, the Germans didn't have it all their own way. By now sonar had been invented, which enabled warships to detect submarines whilst submerged. Just as radar used reflecting radio waves, so sonar used reflecting sound waves. When sound waves arrived back at the ship it was possible to approximate the distance, the depth and the direction of travel of the submarine. Depth charges would them be used to bombard the area, in the hope that the shock waves would crack the hull of the U-boat. The development of sonar meant that U-boats had to quickly escape after making their attacks to avoid being caught in a net of underwater explosions. Sometimes cornered U-boats would pretend to be destroyed by sinking to the seabed and jettisoning oil and cargo as flotsam to create the right impression. They would

then sit for hours in total silence until the enemy decided to move off.

Another interesting development came in the form of dazzle and cryptic camouflage of warships. By painting vessels with inventive patterns and shades it was possible to create optical illusions from a distant viewpoint. The idea was that U-boat commanders would be fooled by what they saw through their periscopes. In some cases camouflage would render vessels invisible, while in other instances ships could be made to look back-to-front or to look like more than one boat in convoy. By confusing the yes, it was hoped that torpedo attacks might be less likely, either for fear of counter attack or wasting torpedoes.

A German U-boat, which was captured in the Atlantic

Russian Navy firing depth charge at German U-boat

U-boats stranded on the south coast of England after surrender

Russian army in snow camouflage advances against the Germans, 1944

Sieges of Leningrad and Stalingrad

During Operation Barbarossa the German Army surrounded the Russian city of Leningrad, but the occupants of the city put up a fierce resistance, so the Germans besieged Leningrad in September 1941. The Germans hadn't bargained on the Russians being so tenacious in their determination to prevent the Germans from taking the city and the siege lasted for almost 900 days, finally ending in Jan 1944 when the Eastern Front was pushed back towards Germany by the Soviet Army.

By the end of the Siege of Leningrad the city lay in ruins, but had never been taken by the Germans because the Russians had established a heavily fortified zone, which formed an impenetrable nucleus. As well as the material cost, the human cost was enormous, with around 1.5 million Russian soldiers and civilians dead. Due to injury, the insanitary conditions and starvation, a further 2.5 million were suffering from illness and disease, but victory belonged to the Soviets.

Leningrad (now St. Petersburg) lies on the coast of the Baltic Sea, to the north of Russia's western border and was strategically desirable to the Germans as a port. Stalingrad (now Volgograd) lies to the south-west of Russia and was strategically desirable because of its industrial facilities and it proximity to the Baku and Maikop oil fields, needed for fuel and lubricants.

German machine gunner on the Russian Front, 1943

German prisoners with soldiers from other Axis satellite countries, huddle against the sharp winds of the Russian winter, after the defeat of the German Army at Stalingrad, February 1943

SCAN WITH
layar
See page 5
for instructions

The Germans launched an extension to Operation Barbarossa in June 1942, named Operation Braunschweig, with the intention of occupying the Caucuses region. In August they reached Stalingrad and the Germans laid siege. This siege was relatively short-lived, lasting for just over six months, but it was no less bloody than the Siege of Leningrad, with hundreds of thousands killed or injured, on both sides.

The Germans came close to defeating the Russians, but the Soviet army managed to surround the enemy while they were focused on taking the city. The successful Soviet offensive was named Operation Uranus. The Germans wanted to make a thrusting assault westward to escape the encirclement, but Hitler ordered the army to stay and fight, believing they could still succeed if the Luftwaffe provided an airborne supply line. He was wrong, as a second Russian winter and heavy anti-aircraft fire prevented the Luftwaffe from reaching the beleaguered German army. The pocket of territory held by the Germans was gradually constricted by the persistent Soviet pressure, until the remaining forces surrendered in February 1943, against Hitler's wishes.

Burmese locals show little interest in the arrival of the Japanese occupying forces in their village, 1942

Burma Campaign

During the Japanese advance of World War II, the Japanese troops cultivated quite a reputation for their hardiness in the field. In the jungles of Burma the Allied forces found life very hard going and were driven out by the Japanese who coped far better with the tropical conditions and therefore had higher morale and better vigour. The Allies were beset with illness, disease, pestilence and fatigue, because they simply didn't know how to look after themselves in the jungle environment. Meanwhile, the Japanese made the most of the natural resources available, keeping themselves well fed, comfortable and free from ailments.

Japanese troops crossing the Salween River to
land at Martaban, during the fall of Rangoon

Lord Louis Mountbatten, British Admiral (Commander-
in-chief of the Allied forces of the Southeast Asia) on the
Front of Burma, March 1944

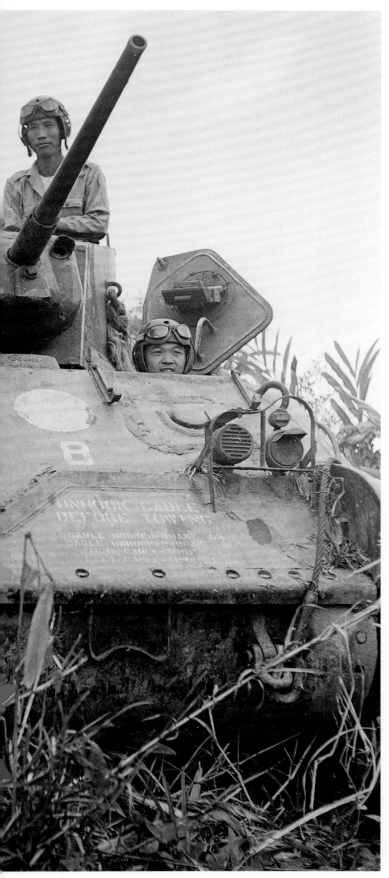

Chinese tank crew on their
American-made M-5 light
tank, Hukawng Valley,
Burma, April 1944

Having been forced to retreat from Burma in early
1942, the Allies then spent two years trying to mount
counter-offensives, but they just couldn't compete
with the Japanese prowess at jungle warfare. In
addition, the Allies learnt to fear the Japanese on a
one-to-one basis, because they were known to charge
at the enemy with a frightening battle cry and an
apparent disregard for their own safety. This was
because the Japanese wanted to die an honourable
death in devotion to their emperor, so they were not
afraid to commit themselves. After a while though,
the Allies realized that the Japanese were quite
frenzied and unfocused in this behaviour, so they were
quiet easy to shoot dead while they charged because
they had no strategy.

In early 1944 the Japanese made a tactical error. They
made a failed attempt to invade India, which left them
depleted of personnel and resources. This marked the
perfect opportunity for the Allies to finally launch a
successful offensive and push the Japanese back out
of Burma.

A similar pattern occurred elsewhere. The Japanese
had invaded the entirety of South-east Asia, but
they stretched themselves too far and allowed the
momentum to shift in favour of the Allies. They found
themselves defending their new empire with ever
depleting manpower and supplies, so retreat to a
smaller area of territory to defend was an inevitable
conclusion. This process was accelerated by the
involvement of the USA as it poured in all it could
to the Allied war effort and developed strategies to
flush the Japanese out of the many occupied islands
in the region.

American aircraft Douglas Dauntless dive-bombers used during great Battle of Midway against Japanese in the Pacific War

Battle of Midway

In June, 1942, the Americans found the Japanese fleet, six months after the Attack on Pearl Harbor, and exacted their revenge. The Japanese had been preparing to attack the Americans at Midway Island, which lies in the North Pacific Ocean roughly halfway between North America and Asia, as its name alludes.

The US force knew the Japanese were somewhere in the area, so they were on the lookout. On the morning of the 4th, a group of US Devastator torpedo bombers located the Japanese and engaged. Most were shot down by the Japanese, but they failed to notice an approaching squadron of thirty-three dauntless dive-bombers dispatched from the USS Enterprise aircraft carrier, and a second squadron of seventeen dauntless dive-bombers from USS Yorktown.

The Japanese defending squadron of Zero fighters had already been scrambled against the Devastators, so they had used their ammunition and were also flying at sea level. When the dive-bombers attacked from above there was nothing the Japanese could do to prevent the US bombs from striking their vessels. Four aircraft carriers were lost to the Americans, along with hundreds of aircraft, and the Japanese no longer had a functioning fleet.

Smoke from antiaircraft guns fills the sky as aircraft carrier USS Yorktown is hit by a Japanese torpedo during the Battle of Midway

The Japanese had gone to Midway with the intention of finishing off the US fleet but been trounced instead. The Americans got lucky on the 4th June, allowing them to tackle the Japanese fleet virtually untouched, due to fortuitous timing. Thus, the USA had its revenge for Pearl Harbor and turned the war in its favour with one fell-swoop.

The Americans were now able to navigate the warzone with relative impunity, as the Japanese could only dispatch aeroplanes from island bases over a limited flight range. The US then set about systematically taking the islands with airstrips, so that the Japanese were progressively restricted in their military movements and in a perpetual state of defence and retreat. In a maritime theatre of war, having naval supremacy meant victory was inevitable for the US, although it would take another three years of ferocious fighting to achieve, such was the Japanese will.

Group photo of the pilots in an American Navy torpedo bomber squadron prior
to the Battle of Midway in which all but one of them would be killed

Women at War

World War II marked a significant gender shift in society. Women made a significant contribution to the war effort in a number of direct and indirect ways. Civilian women worked the land and worked in factories to ensure that rations and resources were made available in large enough quantities to satisfy the basic human-needs of the population. Many other women were trained to manufacture munitions, equipment and machines needed in the theatre of battle. They became highly skilled engineers and technicians, and were often better than their male counterparts because they had a finesse and mindset better suited to the exacting work. By taking on these traditionally male roles, they freed up the men to join the forces, where they could be more useful.

That didn't mean though, that women were not enlisted into the forces. There were many supporting roles within the army, navy and air force that women were able to perform. In fact, they had their own equivalent sections within the forces. In the navy they belonged to the Women's Royal Naval Service (WRNS) otherwise known as the 'Wrens'. In the air force they belonged to the Women's Royal Air Force (WRAF) and were known as 'Wrafs'. In the army, they belonged to the Women's Royal Army Corps (WRAC) and were called 'Wracs'. In these sections they performed all kinds of back-up duties, such as operating supply lines, transporting personnel and equipment, repairs, maintenance and administration. Basically, they did any jobs that weren't considered to place them in situations of high risk at the frontline. That didn't mean they were safe however, as many military women fell victim to bombing raids and so on.

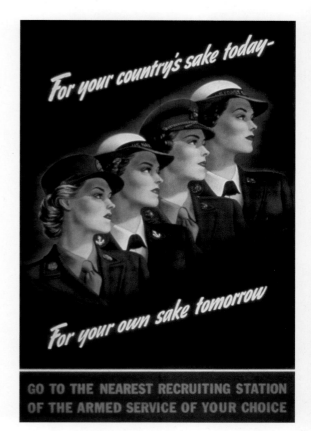

Armed service recruiting poster, 1942

An auxiliary of the US Army

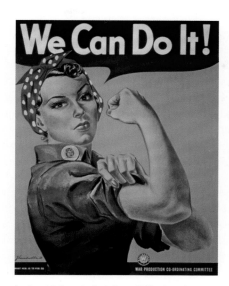

Iconic patriotic poster by J. Howard Miller featuring woman factory worker in bandana rolling up her sleeve & flexing her arm muscles

Indian servicewomen in their traditional saris – they are members of the Women's Royal Naval Service, Women's Auxiliary Army Corps, and the Auxiliary Territorial Service

Women also played an important role in the Royal Army Medical Corps (RAMC) which performed essential work tending the sick and injured in warzones. There was even a Royal Army Dental Corps (RADC) which became officially titled in 1946 in recognition of its value during World War II.

In the WRAF there was a unit called the Air Transport Auxiliary (ATA). This was home to a number of female wartime pilots, whose job it was to deliver and collect military aircraft, so that fighter and bomber squadrons had the serviceable aeroplanes they needed to conduct their missions.

A few women were also involved with the entertainment of troops, as comediennes, singers, dancers and members of musical troupes. Some were music hall celebrities, such a Gracie Fields and Vera Lynn, who would perform with forces orchestras, both in Britain and overseas.

Three female Wren Air mechanics
at a dive bomber station

The Holocaust

It is fair to say that the Nazis had an obsessive hatred for the Jewish race, which became the focal point of their ideology. Historically anti-Semitism was rooted in the fact that Jews were allowed to lend money for profit, which was a practice frowned upon by other religions. In addition, the Jews had been uprooted from their traditional home, which meant that they had to live itinerant lives, travelling around Europe to make their living. They inadvertently cultivated a stereotypical image, as outsiders with strange ways and questionable ethics, who kept themselves to themselves and found advantage in other people's misfortune.

As it is always easier to blame others when the chips are down, Hitler and his cronies found it convenient to target the Jews as responsible for the German hyper-inflation during the Great Depression. While the German population generally struggled to avoid destitution, many Jews seemed to be relatively comfortable, because they existed within a sub-culture. It didn't take much imagination for the Nazis to falsely claim that the Jews had a hand in the fiscal demise of Germany, and it took even less imagination for the general population to believe the Nazis. The power of simple suggestion is potent among people who cannot comprehend the complexity of truth.

The Nazis began their persecution of the Jews by ghettoizing them, to keep them all in one place and out of social circulation. They then began shipping them to remote locations and systematically shooting them, but their scale of ambition was such that they could not process sufficient numbers to keep up with the supply of Jews arriving from all over occupied Europe. This prompted the Nazis to devise more efficient ways of killing Jews and disposing of their remains.

A large group of Jews, escorted by soldiers of the SS, are taken to a concentration camp before the crowds at the roadside

Child survivors of Auschwitz show their
tattooed arms, Poland, February 1945

Nazi leader and war criminal Adolf Eichmann (2nd right)
smiling while German officers cut a Jewish prisoner's hair

In early 1942 Auschwitz, one of the most notorious death camps, began the heinous business of gassing and burning Jews en masse. Any Jews considered useful were housed in a concentration camp and put to labour, while those of no value to the war effort were murdered and incinerated next door. A number of similar camps were constructed to cater for Nazi demand in other regions. The Nazis continued with this ethnic cleansing until the Allies encountered the camps as they advanced across Europe towards Germany. Needless to say, the discovery that the Nazis were capable of such inhumanity to man only fuelled the Allied determination to thoroughly stamp them out of history.

Even to this day, what the Nazis did was so shocking and unspeakable that some people find it hard to believe that it happened. Were it not for the evidence and the witnesses it would indeed be difficult to accept that humans are capable of such horrific crimes against their own species. The way the Nazis engineered the Holocaust was by dehumanizing the Jews to make it easier to commit their wrongs. By removing their clothes and possessions, and shaving their heads, the Nazis removed individuality and personality in the Jews, so that they became a uniform population of clones.

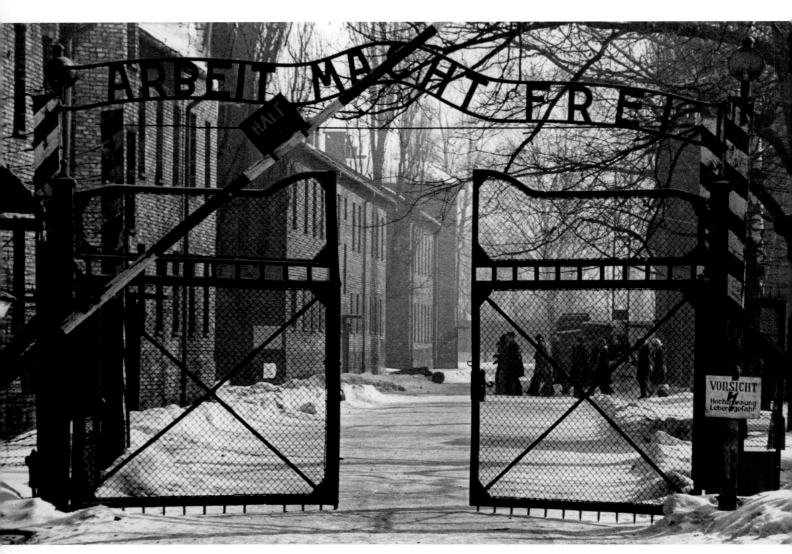

The gates of the Nazi concentration camp at Auschwitz, Poland; the sign above them reads 'Arbeit Macht Frei' - 'Work Makes You Free'

Japanese POWs

While the Nazis' treatment of Jews and other undesirables was despicable, they were relatively less cruel to their POWs in general, although torture and execution were commonplace among prisoners who were suspected of spying against the Third Reich.

The Japanese were the ones who treated their POWs with contempt, because they had the overriding view that all other races were inferior to them. Also, the very idea of surrender or being caught by the enemy went against the Japanese ethos, so those who allowed themselves to become POWs were to be regarded as weak and unworthy of respect. The Japanese would nearly always opt for an honourable death, rather than fall prisoner, and this ideal influenced the way they treated those who chose to remain alive by becoming captive.

British soldiers taken prisoner by the Japanese in Singapore, 1942

The Bataan Death March is one of the most notorious examples of the Japanese treatment of POWs. On April 9th 1942 many US and Filipino prisoners were forced to begin an eighty mile march to the prison camp in which they were to be held, following their capture after the Battle of Bataan. The prisoners were beaten and given insufficient medical care, food and rest, so many died from their injuries, exhaustion and disease along the way. Some were murdered when their condition prevented them from continuing with the journey. There were also a number of death marches from Sandakan to Ranau, in Borneo, where similar treatment of prisoners was standard practice by the Japanese.

For those who survived the death marches, there was worse to come at the hands of those who ran the prison camps. Many were cruelly tortured and starved to death or executed by sword or gun

for no particular reason than the amusement of the Japanese guards and officers, who found their duties tedious and viewed the prisoners as sub-human. In addition to their POW camps, the Japanese also had many internment camps for civilian prisoners, who were also kept in appalling conditions and given woeful treatment.

Many of these civilian prisoners were European colonialists who failed to escape the advancing Japanese. By and large, the native populations of invaded territories were allowed to continue their lives in freedom, although under Japanese occupation, so that they contributed to the war effort. Many indigenous peoples enjoyed a new found liberation from servitude when the Japanese arrived, because their colonial bosses had either fled or been incarcerated. This prompted a general shift towards political independence across the region following the war.

Japanese soldiers march prisoners of war, with arms raised, across the Bataan peninsula in what became known as the Bataan Death March, Luzon, Philippines

Two liberated British POWs from a Japanese prison camp in 1945

Survivors of the Dachau
concentration camp at
the arrival of the VIIth
American army

American troops wading ashore from a landing craft
during the World War II Allied invasion of Italy

Italy Campaign

Winston Churchill described Italy as the soft underbelly of Nazi occupied Europe. The Italians were not renowned for their fighting ability, having been easily beaten back by the Allies in North Africa. Hitler was aware that the Mediterranean coast presented a point of vulnerability, but by 1943 he was occupied with developments on the Eastern Front, and he wasn't entirely sure where the Allies might try their luck at a counter offensive. France offered the most practical landing points, so Axis forces had been stationed along the French coast in anticipation of defensive action.

The Allies went for Italy, precisely because it seemed an unlikely strategic choice and was therefore not defended as well as it might have been. On the 10th July, the Allies mounted an assault of the island of Sicily, to give them a foothold on Italian soil, from where they could launch their offensive of mainland Italy. By the time the Allies were ready for the second phase they had, of course, lost any element of surprise and Hitler had deployed German forces to counter the threat, but the Allied occupation of Sicily was key, as it provided a base for naval, army and air forces. This meant that the Allies could attack with sufficient resources to be certain of making successful landings on the Italian coast.

A group of British soldiers put their shoulders to the side of a stationary truck during the Allied landing in southern Italy.

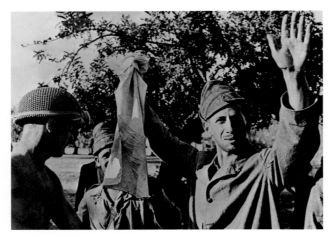

Italian soldiers surrendering after the
landing of allied forces in Sicily

The invasion proper began on 3rd September, with
British troops landing on the 'toe' of the Italian
peninsula. This was called Operation Baytown.
Realizing that the Allies meant business, the Italian
government surrendered on 8th September, but the
Germans intended to fight. The next day, two Allied
invasion forces launched assaults in different regions.
Operation Slapstick hit Taranto, in the 'arch of the foot'
of the Italian Peninsula. The combatants met with little
resistance, as the Germans were expecting an invasion
attempt of the west coast. Meanwhile, Operation
Avalanche struck the beaches of Salerno, on the 'shin'
of the Italian peninsula. Here, the Germans put up
fierce resistance and it took quite a battle for the Allies
to establish a beachhead.

French troops disembark from ships
to occupy the Island of Elba, 1944.

Mussolini's Mistakes

Benito Mussolini rose to power in Italy in 1926, when he seized power as the leader of a fascist regime, in imitation of Adolf Hitler. In 1930 he named himself as Il Duce. Just as Hitler had seduced the Germans with the idea of the Third Reich becoming a new German empire, so Mussolini sold the idea of the 'New Roman Empire' in allusion to the illustrious past of his race.

Things went well for Mussolini until World War II revealed his incompetence as a military tactician, which led the Italian population to turn against him. One major setback was Italy's defeat in North Africa, alongside the Germans, which resulted in the loss of Italian colonial interests. When Operation Barbarossa began on the Eastern Front, Mussolini sent an Italian corps to contribute to the Axis war effort, even though Hitler had not expected the Italians to take part. Mussolini clearly wanted to curry favour with Hitler and have the opportunity to save face by showing that the Italians were a fighting force equal to the Germans. When the tables turned in favour of the Russians, the Italian people were none too impressed by Mussolini's pandering at the expense of many lives.

The scene in a Messina street as a civilian welcomed the arrival of Allied forces in the Sicilian city

Then, when the Allies invaded Sicily, on 10th July, it was the final straw. The Italian industrial infrastructure and home front had taken a battering from Allied bombing, so the population had low morale. Mussolini had tried and failed to persuade Hitler to make peace with the Russians, so that Axis forces could be diverted to Italy to prevent an Allied invasion. Most of the Sicilians actually welcomed the arrival of the Allies and the Italian army was on the point of collapse.

On the night of 24/25th of July, Mussolini was arrested by the Italian military police. The Fascist Grand Council had decided to oust him from power and he was imprisoned. When Hitler learnt of Mussolini's arrest he launched plans for Germany to take control of Italy by arresting the entire government and royal family. The plan was to reinstate Mussolini as a puppet leader, in the interests of the Axis. The Italians then concealed Mussolini's whereabouts from the Germans by moving him about.

On September 12th, Mussolini was rescued from captivity by the Germans. He was then forced, by Hitler, to establish a new fascist regime in northern Italy, named the Italian Social Republic. He remained as puppet leader until April 1945, when he was caught by anti-fascist partisans as he made his way to Switzerland in order to escape to Spain by air. On the 28th he was summarily executed. His body was then hung on display in Milan to satisfy the people that he had got what he deserved, especially for the murder of many Italian partisans.

Mussolini arrested in Rome

Aerial view of the German city of Hamburg
which was heavily bombed by the RAF

Razed to the Ground

In the early hours of the 25th July, 1943, the German city of Hamburg received the first of a series of major bombing raids by the RAF. As the bombers neared their target they released a cloud of foil strips to confuse radar systems, so that the Germans saw only a mass of interference on their screens. Then, in the space of an hour the British dropped 23 hundred tons of bombs across the city. Much of Hamburg was razed to the ground by the bombing, but worse was to come for the inhabitants when the ruined city was engulfed by a firestorm.

It began as a number of small fires left burning after the bombing raid had passed. Conditions happened to be dry, warm and breezy, which allowed the fires to begin spreading. As they met up, there was an exponential increase in heat, so that a conflagration developed. Soon, the convection currents generated by the rising heat were so powerful that air was sucked towards the fire from all directions. The wind was strong enough to suck debris and people into the fire and the surrounding area became so hot with radiation that people were roasted some distance away. Thousands of civilians had been hiding in air raid shelters. They survived the initial bombing but fell victim to the firestorm by succumbing to heat, hypoxia and carbon-monoxide poisoning. Twenty-thousand lost their lives and sixty-thousand were hospitalized.

A solitary figure walking through a devastated area of Hamburg, 1944

A solitary figure walking through a devastated area of Hamburg, 1944

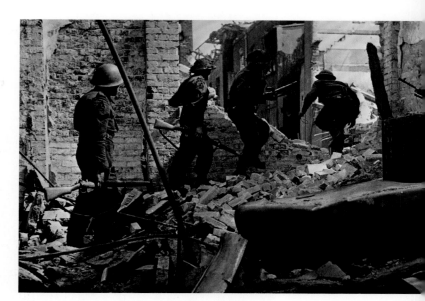

Soldiers from the Royal Ulster Rifles regiment clear a bombed
street as they enter the German city of Bremen

On the 18th November, 1943, it was Berlin's turn to
receive a pounding. The intention was a knockout
blow to the German home front, but German
resistance and tenacity were underestimated. The
bombing campaign lasted until Springtime of 1944,
but still the Germans would not relent. Overall, the
campaign was judged to have failed because it had
not achieved its objective and British losses had
been significant. Over a thousand aircraft and seven
thousand personnel had been lost, with no perceived
gain to the Allies.

Other German cities targeted with bombs include
Bremen and Kiel. Kiel was home to a submarine
base, so the bombing was strategically important.
Similarly, Bremen was home to German shipyards.
The Ruhr industrial region was also subjected to an
intense bombing campaign to knock out steelworks,
oil processing plants, armament factories and so on.
The bombings lasted from March to July 1943 and
greatly hindered Germany's ability to manufacture
the equipment and resources it needed for its war
effort. It was all part of the attrition needed to ensure
that the Allied landings in Italy and France would
stand a chance of success.

A scene at what was Potsdam Station, Berlin – the station was hit in four heavy bombing raids, two by the RAF and two by the US Air Force

The V-1 was a form of unguided missile developed by the Germans in World War II, it was knick named the 'doodlebug', 'or buzz bomb'

Operation Crossbow

Fastidious aerial reconnaissance by British intelligence had revealed that the Germans were developing secret weapons. In 1943 Operation Crossbow was initiated as a counter measure to these developments. Photographs betrayed the existence of mysterious objects and installations in various locations, in Germany and France. At first British command didn't quite know what to make of interpretations of the photographs, because they were taken from above at altitude. There was uncertainty about what the pictures showed, and there was uncertainty about whether they were real or just decoys designed to fool the Allies into launching wasted bombing raids.

However, images from a site at Peenemünde on the German Baltic coast convinced the Allies that the Germans were indeed working on advanced weaponry. Outlines and shadows suggested flying weapons of one kind or another and indicated that German technology was more advanced than that of the Allies.

The evidence was sufficient to launch Operation Hydra, as part of Crossbow, on the 17th August, which was a strategic bombing raid of the Peenemünde site. The Allies had been correct in their assessment of the evidence, as the site was where the German V-2 Rocket was being prototyped and the V-1 flying bomb was undergoing test flights.

A city street is littered with the corpses of Belgian civilians and soldiers after the explosion of a German V-1 flying bomb

Injured civilians are assisted by rescue
workers after a German V-2 rocket exploded
in Farringdon Road, London, 1945

The bombing set developments back and caused the
scientists and engineers to relocate, but it also made
it clear that the Allies were wise to the V-weapons
programmes. In the long-term it meant that the
Allies could do little to prevent the V-1 and V-2 from
being perfected by the Germans and then being mass
produced and used in anger against them.

As Operation Crossbow continued into 1944, attention
turned to the launch sites for the weapons, which
were being constructed all over north-western
Europe. The V-1 used a conspicuous launch ramp and
the weapons were housed in hockey-stick shaped
sheds, making them fairly easy to spot and destroy.
The V-2 was more problematic as it had a longer range
and required only a portable launch pad, making it
undetectable prior to use. However, the Germans had
initially intended to store and launch V-2 rockets
from a heavily fortified bunker called La Coupole
(The Dome), at the northern tip of France.

It was so heavily bombed by the Allies in the Summer
of 1944 that the Germans were forced to abandon the
site before its completion.

After their surrender, a group of German V-2 rocket scientists
pose with members of the US 7th Army, 44th Infantry Division,
near Oberammergau, Germany, May 2, 1945

Tunisia Campaign

On 13th May, 1943, Winston Churchill received a message, reading "The Tunis campaign is over. All enemy resistance has ceased. We are masters of the North African shores." The news came two months prior to the Allied invasion of Sicily, where the war was about to be taken from Africa to continental Europe. It marked the beginning of the end for the Axis powers.

Before World War II, Tunisia was a French protectorate, with 250,000 French and Italian colonists. It became the last remaining enclave for the Axis powers after a series of North African battles and the Allied campaign to finally defeat the enemy outright began on 17th November 1942.

Initially the combined German and Italian force did well, but the Allies had the logistical advantage. They had open supply lines to keep equipment,

provisions and personnel pouring into the theatre of battle, so it was just a matter of time before the Axis force was cornered in the city of Tunis and faced with annihilation or surrender - they chose the latter.

Some military historians regard the Tunisia Campaign as one of the tactical errors that led to the demise of the Nazi regime. Hitler's motive for sending in so many German troops was to keep the Mediterranean under Axis control, so that an Allied invasion remained impracticable. In reality it only delayed the inevitable by six or so, and it cost Hitler dearly in terms of available manpower and resources. He would have been better off by evacuating North Africa and consolidating his defenses on the European Mediterranean coast.

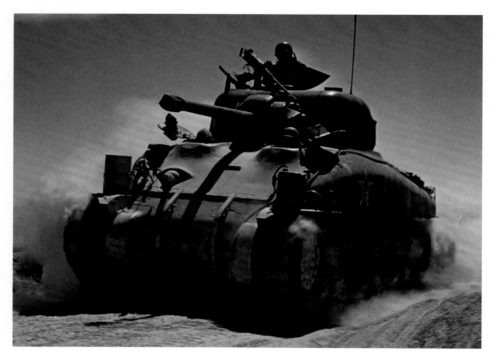

American M4 Sherman tank racing along during the desert fighting between US and German forces in the El Guettar Valley

German troops after the capture of Tebourba, Tunisia, 1942

In hindsight, it is possible that he may have successfully beaten the Allies back from Italy in September 1943, but that is a matter of pure conjecture. After all, he was also in the process of stretching the Axis too far on the Eastern Front. Fundamentally, Hitler's ambitions of conquest got the better of his common sense, because he wasn't guided or motivated by military strategic thinking. He wanted too much too soon, so that he could live up to the promise he had made to the German people, and in his haste to demonstrate his omnipotence he made basic errors of judgement, so blinded by his ego that he could not listen to the advice offered by his military commanders.

A B25 bomber taking off from the USS
Hornet on a bombing raid of Tokyo

Royal Air Force flying in loose formation
over the Tunisian desert providing cover
for Allied bombers, April 1943

Pacific Sweep

Following the Battle of Midway, in 1942, the
Japanese were limited in their ability to
defend their interests, making it easier for the
Allies to begin the process of pushing the invaders
back towards their own archipelago. Nevertheless, it
wasn't going to be an easy process, because Japan's
territorial gains comprised a great many islands of
different sizes, so that each required its own battle
on one scale or another. Also, the Allies would need
to mount assaults from sea to land, making them
extremely vulnerable to defensive fire while the
Japanese were concealed in networks of tunnels,
trenches and bunkers on higher ground.

When the Americans began their sweep of the
Pacific islands they knew that the holed-up Japanese
garrisons were isolated by the retreat of the Japanese
force as a whole. This meant, it was a matter of
attrition in order to take each island. The Americans
began by bombarding an island with shells fired from
warships placed some distance away, and bombs
dropped by aircraft, whilst the landing party prepared
to make their assault and establish a beachhead.

Japanese kamikaze putting on his forehead
bandeau with rising sun, 1944

Despite efforts to destroy enemy positions, the
Japanese would often survive in significant
numbers and have sufficient weaponry to put up
fierce resistance. So, the Americans had to adopt a
systematic approach to flushing the Japanese from
their lairs. This involved the use of flamethrowers
and grenades to either kill or force the Japanese into
the open. They were usually shot as they emerged,
because they were inclined to have one last attempt
at aggression in order to die honourably. Very few
surrendered themselves to the Americans, as that
was considered such a shameful way to behave.

On the larger islands of Southeast Asia, the situation
was rather different, because the theatre of battle
was tropical jungle, which presented a different
set of problems. In particular, there was the lack of
visibility in the thick vegetation. This meant that
platoons of Allied and Japanese troops would fall
upon one another by chance and enter into battle at
close quarters, often involving hand-to-hand combat.
In both types of situation, casualty numbers were
high, but the Allies gradually and methodically swept
the Japanese back to whence they had come. As the
circumference of the Japanese held territory reduced
however, then the easier it became for them to
defend it, so the fighting became progressively
more fierce the farther it moved towards the
Japanese archipelago.

View of the USS North Carolina
battleship en route in the Pacific Ocean

Infantrymen of the US 8th Army pour ashore in the Subic Bay area
of Luzon Island in the northern Philippines, en route to Manila

Anzio and Cassino

In January 1944 the Allies had fought their way up the Italian peninsula to a line above Naples and below Rome, called the Gustav Line. The line ran through the town of Cassino on the route to Rome, which was held by the Germans. The town lay in the shadow of a rocky mount named Monte Cassino, which gave the Germans the advantage of high ground. The Allies were faced with a ferocious battle against the Axis in order to continue their journey northwards.

On the 22nd January the Allies mounted Operation Shingle, which was a new phase of beach landings on the western Italian at Anzio, just above the Gustav Line. This was a strategic offensive designed to present a threat to the Gustav Line from both sides. The Germans were taken by surprise and 50,000 Allied troops had come ashore by the following day. However, the high command were too cautious to venture inland without the delivery of tanks and artillery, and this gave the Germans the chance to reorganize themselves in defence.

Although the landings were successful in establishing a new foothold on the Italian coast, the ensuing battle turned out to be costly for the Allies. The intention of outflanking the Germans at Monte Cassino was abandoned due to the weight of resistance and the terrain, but the army gradually worked its way north to Rome. This became known as the Anzio breakout, and was made possible by fooling the Germans into thinking that a sea landing would be made near Rome. In anticipation of these landings, German high command redeployed in that area, leaving a point of defensive weakness, which the Anzio troops were able to exploit.

An American soldier landing on the beaches of Anzio, Italy, 50Km south of Rome on January 22, 1944

American troops dock at the port of Anzio during the Allied invasion of Italy known as Operation Shingle

The German 10th Army, which the Allies had hoped to ensnare, ultimately managed to escape the trap by making a fighting retreat northwards, when they realized that Cassino was lost to the Allies. By the time Allied forces reached Rome, the Germans had strategically evacuated the city. In a haunting echo of World War I, the town of Cassino was razed to the ground by shells and bombs, so that it was a field of rubble with the occasional ruin still standing. Above the town, on the mount, there had been a monastery, but it was entirely destroyed by the Allies who mistakenly believed that the Germans had fortified the building in readiness for the battle.

Battle of Kursk: A German
Panzer VI Tiger between
Bielgorod and Orel, July 1943

The Russian War Machine

The turning point for the Eastern Front came with the Battle of Kursk in the summer of 1943. The battle was so costly to the Axis that they were no longer able to prevent the Russians from advancing westward. It had been so costly because the Germans were still in a weakened position following the Russian winter, and they were effectively forced to stand their ground to avoid the advance of the newly optimistic Russians. In anticipation of a German offensive, the Russians had dug themselves into a fortified line, which comprised a remarkable 3750 miles of trenches, nearly a thousand observation and command posts and 48 thousand positions for artillery and mortars.

Battle of Kursk: A German Panzer VI Tiger between Bielgorod and Orel, July 1943

The Russians had built an impenetrable barrier. They also had 2.5 million troops, while the Germans had less than 1 million. The also had almost 8,000 tanks, to the Germans' 3,000. They also had 2,800 aircraft, while the Germans had 2,100. And they had 25,000 guns and mortars against the Germans' 10,000. Needless to say, the odds were stacked heavily against the Germans from the off.

The Russians allowed the Germans to exhaust themselves with the futility of attempting to breach the fortified line and then launched counter-offensives. In terms of losses, the Germans faired far better than the Russians, because they were a far better fighting force, but the battle was a decisive victory for the Russians simply because combative attrition had crippled the German force, which was forced into retreat. Sheer strength in numbers had given the Russians the upper hand,

and that is how things remained for the rest of the war.

By the springtime of 1944, the Russians had retaken the Ukraine and were well on their way to pushing the Germans back across Eastern Europe. The Third Reich was steadily constricting from the east and from the south. Soon it would be constricting from the West too, as the Allies were planning a mass invasion of German occupied France, so that Hitler's empire could be dissolved and eroded from all sides. The Russian army was particularly shocked by discovering the way the Nazis had treated the Russians under their occupation and this resentment grew as they closed in on the regime. Prospects were very grim for any Nazis who were caught by the Russians.

Germans in the Ukraine making their escape from the approaching Russians

A German soldier sitting with his head in his hands by a destroyed heavy artillery gun following the Battle of Kursk

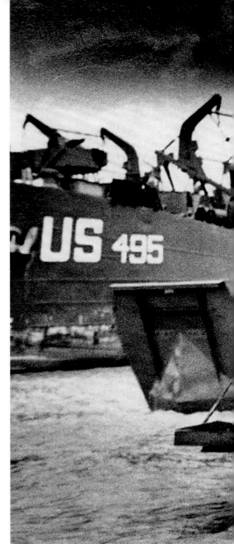

American soldiers disembarking from an LCI landing craft upon its arrival on the beaches of Normandy for Operation Overlord

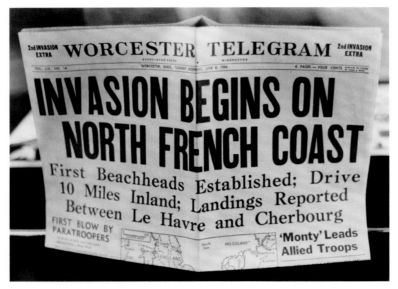

Newspapers reporting the Allied invasion of Normandy on D-Day, 6th June 1944

Plans for Invasion

In order to achieve a successful invasion of Nazi-occupied France it was necessary for the Allies to organize Operation Overlord in as much secrecy as possible. However, it was impossible to conceal the vast build-up of troops and military equipment necessary for the offensive. This meant that the only real secrets were the time and location of the invasion, so the Allies played this to their advantage.

As the shortest route across the English Channel was between Dover and Calais, the Allies decided to work on the idea that Hitler could be persuaded that this was the intention if they used every trick in the book to deceive Hitler.

Decoy tanks and aircraft were positioned near to the Dover coast to fool German reconnaissance into

believing that invasion preparations were under way. Some decoys were fabricated from wood and canvas, others were inflatable rubber, but they appeared very convincing from a bird's eye view. False radio messages were also transmitted, so that German intelligence sent erroneous information to Hitler.

Meanwhile, efforts were made to conceal the genuine invasion preparation activity going on at or near a number of ports farther to the west on the English south coast. The troops themselves were kept in the dark about the details of the invasion. They were housed at barracks inland, so that they had no idea where they would embark on the fateful day.

American Sherman tanks and troops move through the damaged and bombed town of Flere as they move inland from the Normandy beach

The timing of the invasion was not fixed, due to the requirement for clement weather conditions. This meant that everything needed to be able to be held on standby and ready to put into operation at short-notice, as and when high command pressed the green light.

Despite the odds against keeping the plans covert, Hitler remained uncertain about the Allies' plans and decided to keep the majority of his defensive force in the Calais area. When the invasion came in Normandy there was still fierce resistance from the Germans, but nowhere near as much as there would have been had Hitler second-guessed the Allies' plans.

In addition, Erwin Rommel happened to be away on leave, so that German defenses were not commanded efficiently. Several Panzer divisions could have been deployed with devastating effect, but Hitler had refused to move them far enough west and Rommel was about to persuade him to do so. As it was, the tanks were too far east, and Rommel was not on the scene quickly enough to orchestrate any measures to prevent the Allies from securing a firm foothold.

German Prisoners of War (POW) have been put behind barbed wire on
Omaha Beach where American invasion forces landed 6th June, 1944

D-Day

The first day of Operation Overlord came on 6th June, 1944. It was called D-Day, or Zero-Day, so that each subsequent day had a number: D plus 1, D plus 2, and so on. The idea was that certain objectives were met in rapid succession following the landings, to make sure that Germans were unable to mount a counter offensive and keep the momentum on the side of the Allies.

The landing troops embarked on their journey across the English Channel during the night of the 5-6th June. There had been a storm on the 5th and further storms were forecast, so high command had opted to go for a short window in the weather, rather than wait any longer and risk the Germans finding out.

The beaches of Normandy had been given five code names; Utah, Omaha, Gold, Juno, and Sword, running west to east. The fleet assembled mid-channel, having sailed from various locations in southern England and Wales, and then headed for their fate with destiny. A number of airborne Paratroop units had gone ahead to attack German defensive positions and take bridges near the town of Caen, to prevent the enemy from deploying reserve forces farther west.

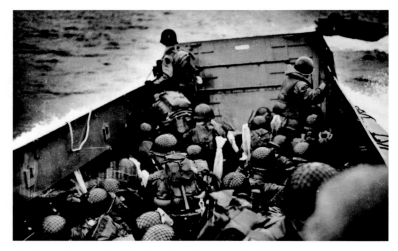

American soldiers aboard an LCI landing craft on its way across the English Channel towards the beaches of Normandy for Operation Overlord

Soldiers of the 3rd Canadian Infantry Division have set up anti-aircraft guns on Juno Beach where they landed on D-Day

When the landing parties begin their assaults, they were met with varying difficulties, due to the different geography and defensive installations. Omaha beach, for example, was backed by steep cliffs, with machine gun positions at a vantage point. Troops had to rush to the foot of the cliffs and wait until the defences had been destroyed. Utah beach, as it was farthest west, was only poorly defended. The troops had relatively little trouble in establishing a safe beachhead. Elsewhere, resistance was fierce, but the Germans were unable to prevent the Allies from coming ashore and defeating them.

Utah and Omaha beaches were assigned to the US First Army. Sword and Gold beaches were assigned to the British Second Army, and Juno beach was assigned to the Canadian Second Infantry Division. By the evening of the 6th, all five beach zones were safely in Allied hands and the armies had met up with the airborne divisions inland. The next phase of the attack was to consolidate the Allies' position by taking Cherbourg, to the west, and Caen, to the east, before beginning the invasion proper and forcing German lines back towards central Europe.

Meanwhile, there was the matter of supply lines. As the Normandy beaches offered no ports for transport ships to moor up, the Allies used prefabricated floating harbors called 'Mulberries'. They comprised floating section that ran out into deep water, so that vehicles could disembark by driving along a gangway and then use ramps to come ashore. In this way, the Allies managed to off-load all of the military hardware and reserve troops they required in a short space of time, to keep the frontline constantly moving.

SCAN WITH
layar
See page 5
for instructions

US troops march up beachhead
while landing craft in rear continue to
unload supplies, equipment and men
following victorious D-Day invasion

The French heroes of D-Day in Quistreham, France on June 06, 1944

The Push

On D-Day the Allied force numbered 156,000, while the Germans had just 10,000. By the end of the day, 12,000 Allies had lost their lives against the German defensive positions, but the prime objective of Operation Overlord had been achieved. The Germans lost between and half and two-thirds of their men, while the rest were either taken prisoner or managed to retreat.

The subsequent fight to begin pushing the Germans eastward was not going to be easy. Allied high command had been hopeful of bringing the war to an end before the close of 1944, but the Germans had other ideas. The ceasefire of World War I had seen the Allies and Germans leave the field of battle in France and Belgium. This time, the Germans knew they would be chased all the way back to Berlin, so they put up an incredibly fierce resistance all of the way across Western Europe. Also, as the perimeter of the Third Reich gradually shrank, the German forces had less frontline to defend, so their resistance was undiminishing. As a result, many battles ensued as the Germans made tactical retreats to natural obstacles, such as rivers, where they stood their ground.

German soldiers captured during the Battle of Normandy

273

Despite their best efforts to keep the Allies from advancing, they inevitably failed because of the same logistical imbalance that had been their undoing on the Eastern Front. The Allies had an inexhaustible supply of equipment and reserve troops, while the Germans had finite and diminishing resources. Of course, the German high command knew very well that the situation was hopeless and wanted to sue for peace before the Allies invaded Germany, but Hitler flatly refused to consider surrender as an option. In fact, it seems that he grew so obsessed with the idea that Germany was 'meant' to win the war, that he wouldn't listen to his military officers. So, the war at the Western Front continued despite the eventual outcome being quite obvious.

In Italy, the Allies had reached the Gothic Line, well above Rome and on the Eastern Front, the Russians had entered Poland. It was only a matter of time before Hitler's domain was reduced in size to a smaller area than he had started with. In Asia the Japanese were being pushed out of China and Burma, and in Southeast Asia they were being steadily purged from the many islands. The wars in both the West and in the East were both going well for the Allies and badly for the Axis.

Soldiers of the 5th Allied Army pass a dead German soldier as they push their way through the enemy's mountainous Gothic line of defence in Italy

V-Weapons

Following the Normandy landings on the 6th June 1944, part of the German's defensive strategy was to unleash their secret weapons, the V-1 flying bomb and the V-2 rocket bomb, in an attempt to make the Allies think twice about advancing.

The first V-1 was launched on the 13th June, just a week after D-Day. Between June and October over 9.5 thousand V-1s were fired at London and other parts of Southeast England. Eventually the launch sites were overrun by the Allies as they advanced eastward, so the Germans were only able to continue firing them at targets in Belgium, because the V-1 had a limited range. 12,000 V-1s were successfully launched, but they killed a relatively low number of civilians, at just short of 23,000. With fewer than two casualties per bomb, they had no persuasive effect on the Allies, but they did have a psychological impact. This was partly because the V-1 was propelled by a noisy pulse-jet engine, which would cut-out to allow the bomb to fall. The abrupt end to the noise struck fear into people, because the exact point of contact with the ground was random, so it was matter of waiting for the sound of the explosion.

A V-1 rocket or flying bomb, in flight over the city of London, 1943

The V-2 rocket bomb was a different matter altogether. It flew at supersonic speed, so no one heard or saw it coming. There would be a sudden and unexpected explosion as the ballistic missile struck the ground from a high trajectory. The first of over 3 thousand V-2s was launched on 8th September. They killed an average of about three people, because there was no prior warning of a strike and they carried larger warheads.

The V-1 was essentially an unmanned, or drone, aeroplane. As it was visible, noisy and slow-flying at low altitude, it was fairly easy to shoot down with antiaircraft guns or to intercept with fighter aircraft. The V-2, on the other hand, was state of the art technology and the Allies had no way to counter the threat, apart from preventing it from being launched in the first place. Although the V-2 was a remarkable machine for its time, it was enormously expensive to manufacture. Each V-2 cost the same as a fighter plane, and each V-1 about half that, so Hitler would have been far wiser to have invested in 9 thousand aircraft, which would have been far more effective in defending the Western Front.

Canadian soldiers sitting on a German V-1 bomb
which failed to reach its target in Britain

The aftermath of a V1
'doodlebug' flying bomb
attack, England, 1944

Devastation caused by
German V1 'doodlebug' in
South London, 1944

The Plot Against Hitler

In July, 1944, only the Nazi party faithful still believed that Hitler could win the war. With the Allies back in France and advancing steadily east, most of the German high command knew the game was up. So, they hatched a plot to assassinate the Fuhrer and then negotiate a peace treaty. A number of partisan assassination attempts had failed over the years, as Hitler was careful to make his behaviour varied and unpredictable, but this time it seemed that the plot could not fail.

On the 20th July, a conspirator named Claus von Stauffenberg attended one of Hitler's military conferences, carrying a bomb concealed in a suitcase. Having planted the bomb beneath the table where Hitler would be standing, Stauffenberg was summoned away to a planned telephone call before the blast was detonated. The explosion wrecked the conference room, but Hitler had survived because the wide leg of the table had shielded him from the blast. He was injured, but not mortally, and immediately set about rounding up the conspirators for execution. Meanwhile, the conspirators had been so confident that Hitler must have died in the explosion, that they revealed themselves by prematurely implementing the next stage of their plan. In so doing, they signed their own death warrants, and Hitler had a much better idea of whom he could trust.

German General Erwin von Witzleben, who was involved in the July Plot to assassinate Hitler – he was tried, found guilty of treason and hanged in 1944

Dr Carl Friedrich Goerdeler, Burgermeister of Leipzig, on trial for his participation in the 'July Plot' to assassinate Hitler

Erwin Rommel, who was blackmailed
by Hitler into taking his own life

Erwin Rommel had agreed to lend his support to the
conspiracy against Hitler, which was already afoot
in the springtime of 1944. At the time of the bombing
Rommel was recovering from battle injuries, but he
was clearly implicated. As Rommel was the most
popular officer in the German army, Hitler had a
problem to solve. If he had Rommel executed and
declared a traitor, then it would cause low morale at
the Western Front or even initiate mutiny amongst
the army with the knowledge that Rommel had
lost faith in Hitler. To avoid a possible coup, Hitler
decided to inform Rommel that his family and friends
would be murdered unless he committed suicide. So
Rommel took a cyanide pill on October 14th 1944. The
official version of events was that Rommel had either
suffered a heart attack or a brain haemorrhage due to
the head injuries he had sustained in July.

A German soldier sits amongst the ruins of the Reichstag in Berlin after the Russian army entered the city in 1945

Allies at the Gates

On the 29th April, 1945, the German army in Italy surrendered to the Allies. Since the autumn of 1944, the Allied and Axis forces had been in a stalemate, but on the 8th April, 1945, the German frontline began to give way. The Germans made a number of tactical retreats but decided to throw in the towel just three weeks later. This was the start of the closing chapter for the Third Reich.

Only three days prior to the German surrender on the Italian front, the Russians had surrounded Berlin and begun their assault on the German capital, where Hitler and his cronies were holed up. On the 20th April, Hitler had celebrated his 56th birthday, undoubtedly aware that it would be his last. Nevertheless, he resolutely kept on barking orders to the army units defending Berlin, determined that Germany would sink in a ball of flames rather than surrender.

A German soldier sits amongst the ruins of the Reichstag in Berlin after the Russian army entered the city in 1945

People crowd on top of a van during VE
Day celebrations, London, 8th May 1945

As the Battle of Berlin progressed, the tactics were adapted to street warfare, where every building had to be purged of Nazi resistance. As a result, many civilians died in the crossfire, also, the Russians were in no mood to distinguish between the two, as a German was a Nazi was a German in their view. They had seen evidence of the Nazis inhumanity to man on countless occasions as the Eastern Front had moved west, and sympathy was not an emotion forthcoming. Many Berlin women were raped by the Russians as a gesture of humiliation and revenge.

When the Nazis realized what they could expect at the hands of the Russians, many travelled west to surrender to the Americans and British, knowing they would have a better chance of survival.

Herman Goering, who had fled to Bavaria, telegrammed Hitler to suggest that he took over the leadership, since the Fuhrer was indisposed

and unlikely to escape the Russian encirclement. Hitler was furious but powerless to retaliate. On the 28th April he was informed that his army had only two days' worth of ammunition left, so Hitler resigned himself to his fate. He married his mistress Eva Braun on the 29th and both committed suicide on the 30th. Admiral Karl Dönitz succeeded Hitler until Germany officially surrendered to the Allies on 23 May 1945.

VE (Victory in Europe) day was celebrated on 7-8th of May, as that was when hostilities ceased and Allied nations realized that peace had finally arrived after nearly six years of war. However, hostilities had not yet ceased in Asia, where the Japanese were still putting up a spirited and fanatical resistance.

Crowds in Piccadilly Circus celebrate VE Day

In his last official photo, Adolf Hitler leaves the safety of his bunker
to award decorations to members of Hitler Youth, February, 1945

Iwo Jima and Okinawa

As the Americans fought their way nearer to the Japanese archipelago, the enemy battled ever more ferociously. Surrender was not an option for the Japanese mindset, as it was better to die honourably at arms or to commit suicide to avoid the shame of being held prisoner. There was also the incentive of protecting their homeland and the Japanese civilian population. The Japanese army judged the Allies by their own standards and presumed that their people would be harshly treated if they were defeated, so they had every reason to fear their enemy and to fight maniacally to the end. The battles of Iwo Jima and Okinawa have gone down in the annals of history as two of the bloodiest campaigns ever fought.

The Battle of Iwo Jima lasted from February 19th to March 26th 1945. The Allies wanted to take Iwo Jima as a staging post to mount airborne attacks on the Japanese main islands. The prospect of the Americans getting that close to Japan gave the Japanese a resolve that made them very hard to fight. The Japanese force numbered nearly 22,000 and all died bar just 216 who were taken prisoner. More than 99% of the Japanese troops were killed by the Americans before Iwo Jima was secured. This statistic would be very telling in decisions to come about how to win the war.

Soldiers raising the United States flag
at Iwo Jima, February 23, 1945

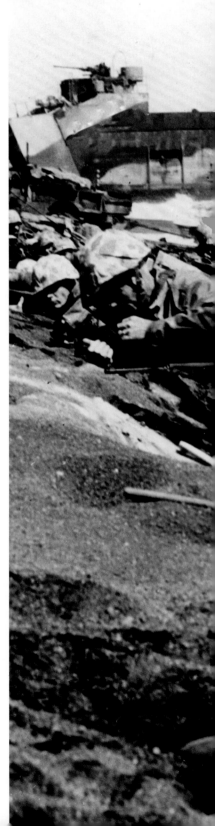

US Marines lying on the beach
of Iwo Jima bombarded by
Japanese artillery

An American
serviceman shares
his rations with two
Japanese children in
Okinawa, Japan, 1945

American soldier under fire of Japanese machine
guns in the Death Valley where 125 US soldiers
were killed in May 1945 in Okinawa, Japan

It was a similar story with the Battle of Okinawa,
fought between April 1st and June 22nd 1945. The
Japanese also made use of a kamikaze flying bomb,
called the Ohka, which was much like the German
V-1, except that it was piloted by a human volunteer,
so that it could be aimed precisely at targets, which
were usually American ships. The idea of making
a certain sacrificing of one's life for the sake of the
war effort was alien and disturbing to the Allies, as
is indicated a level of fanaticism in the Japanese,
suggesting that they would stop at nothing. They
also had a kamikaze submarine, called the kaiten,
and began using standard aircraft for suicidal
bombing missions.

By the time Iwo Jima and Okinawa were in US hands
it was clear that a great many more Americans and
Japanese would die if it were necessary to take the
war to Japan itself. As the Japanese were not about
to surrender or to agree to a ceasefire, the Allies
had no choice but to continue their advance until a
conclusion was met.

Atomic Bomb

Behind the scenes during World War II, the Allies had grown increasingly concerned that the Nazis and the Japanese might be developing nuclear weapons, for it was known that they were experimenting with nuclear technologies. As it happened their scientists had abandoned ideas of atomic weapons before Germany surrendered, but the US had initiated a nuclear weapons program in New Mexico, named the Manhattan Project.

On July 16th 1945, the US scientists conducted their first atomic bomb test, called the Trinity Test. It was an unqualified success and it immediately became apparent that the Americans had a terrifying new weapon that might be deployed against the Japanese to end the remaining war in the Far East.

The decision to go ahead and use the atomic bomb against Japan was not made lightly and was based on a balance of statistics. It was calculated that a continuation of conventional warfare would kill a quarter of a million Americans and several million Japanese. Although the atomic bomb might kill hundreds of thousands, it was hoped that it would force the Japanese to capitulate, so that overall losses were far fewer.

The first of two atomic bombs was dropped on the city of Hiroshima on August 6th 1945, and was named 'Little Boy'. On detonation, two pieces of uranium were fired together to create a critical mass, leading to nuclear chain reaction and a single explosion with sufficient force to annihilate the entire city.

American bomber pilot Paul W. Tibbets Jr. (centre) stands with the ground crew of the bomber 'Enola Gay', which Tibbets flew in the atomic bombing of Hiroshima

A dense column of smoke rises more than 60,000 feet into the air over the Japanese industrial port of Nagasaki, the result of an atomic bomb

The second atomic bomb was dropped on the city of Nagasaki on August 9th 1945 and was named 'Fat Man'. This bomb worked on a different principle, which was also used for the Trinity Test. A sphere of plutonium was surrounded by a shell of conventional explosive, so that detonation caused the plutonium to increase in density and initiate a nuclear chain reaction.

There had been two designs just in case one hadn't worked on the day. In fact, both worked with such devastating effect that the Japanese announced their intention to surrender just five days later. VJ (Victory over Japan) Day was celebrated 14-15th August and the surrender was signed on September 2nd.

It has been estimated that the Hiroshima and Nagasaki bombs killed around a quarter of a million civilians, either in the initial blasts of from injuries and the effects of radiation. It remains a matter of conjecture as to whether that figure would have been exceeded by a conventional conclusion to the war, but it seems likely that it would when considering the Japanese determination to fight or die. Certainly fewer American lives were lost and Japan suffered relatively little collateral damage too.

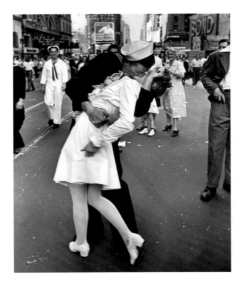

US servicemen celebrate their return home in Times Square following the long awaited-victory over Japan

The ruins after the atomic bomb attack on Hiroshima

A group of political prisoners held at the Dachau concentration camp by the Nazi's for their opposition to the German regime

The Shape of Things to Come

During World War II, the Nazi regime made a systematic attempt to eradicate the Jewish race from Europe. Approximately 6 million Jews died in the Holocaust. When the Allies liberated the death camps there was universal condemnation of what the Nazis had done. Not least because it became apparent what humans were capable of doing to other humans in the name of ideology and belief. People preferred to think that the savage side of humanity had been left behind in our prehistory. The Nazis showed that it was still there, lying dormant and ready to rear its ugly head when humans were susceptible to the power of suggestion and persuasion.

This collective enlightenment about the true nature of the human condition seemed to generate a reaction against it, in an effort to ensure that the circumstances for its germination never arose again. From this storm of shock and disappointment in humanity came the idea for a Jewish nation, as compensation for their treatment and a way of salving the conscience of the Allies, as much as the defeated Germans, who recognized that anti-Semitism was really the fault of all.

So, in 1947 the United Nations General Assembly approved the idea of giving the Jews their own homeland, and in 1948 the State of Israel was formed. Unfortunately, it required the partitioning of Palestine, which displaced another population who had lived there for countless generations. Thus, the Israeli Jews have still never known peace and security, because acquiring the land has led to a whole new set of problems.

Goering on trial for war crimes in 1946

As for the Germans, they had to take a long hard look at themselves after the war. Many civilians had either participated in the persecution to some extent, or turned a blind eye to what was going on. There was a general sense of shame that the Nazis had been allowed to take things so far, which led to the unfortunate phenomenon of Holocaust denial. It was easier to deny the truth, despite the overwhelming evidence, by claiming that the evidence was all part of an elaborate conspiracy to discredit the Nazis. That, in itself, provides some idea of just how horrific and unspeakable the Nazi crimes against humanity were.

Following the Nuremburg trials, after the war, many Nazi leaders were executed for their decisions and behavior, which had little or nothing to do with the concept of legitimate warfare, as described by the Geneva Convention. Nazi hunters, bent on revenge and justice, spent decades in pursuit of those Nazis who had managed to escape abroad.

An Independent World

For different reasons, many European colonies, in Asia and Southeast Asia, began a drive for independence following World War II. For some, it was the feeling that they had sacrificed personnel only because they had been ordered to by the colonial powers and had gained nothing in return. For others, it was because falling under Axis control had not been such a bad experience, as they had been given their autonomy for a few years. As a result the world map began to change considerably in the post-war era.

In marked contrast, other countries lost their autonomy, because they were absorbed into the newly formed Soviet Union. Although the Russians had been among the Allies during the war, this was only a nominal status in real terms. The truth was that the Russians were the enemies of Germany, just as the Britain, France and the USA were, but that is where the alliance stopped. Having been the first to Berlin, the Russians wanted a decent sized chunk of Europe as their reward.

It was difficult to argue against, since the Russians had lost about twenty million people on the Eastern Front, so Stalin got what he wanted. East Germany, Poland, Czechoslovakia, Hungary, Romania and Bulgaria all became satellite states of the Soviet Union, as the Communist Bloc.

Communist-Socialist
Bloc meeting, 1947

West Berliners peering through
the Berlin Wall into the Eastern
sector near Check Point Charlie

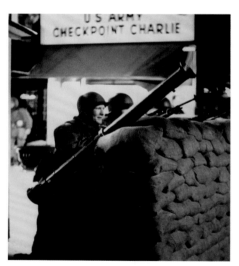

US on guard at Checkpoint
Charlie, Berlin wall

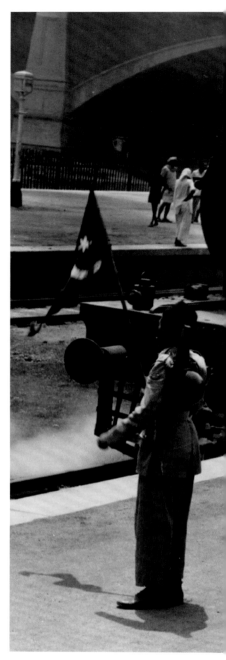

30 special trains leaving
New Delhi Station which will
take the staff of the Pakistan
government to Karachi

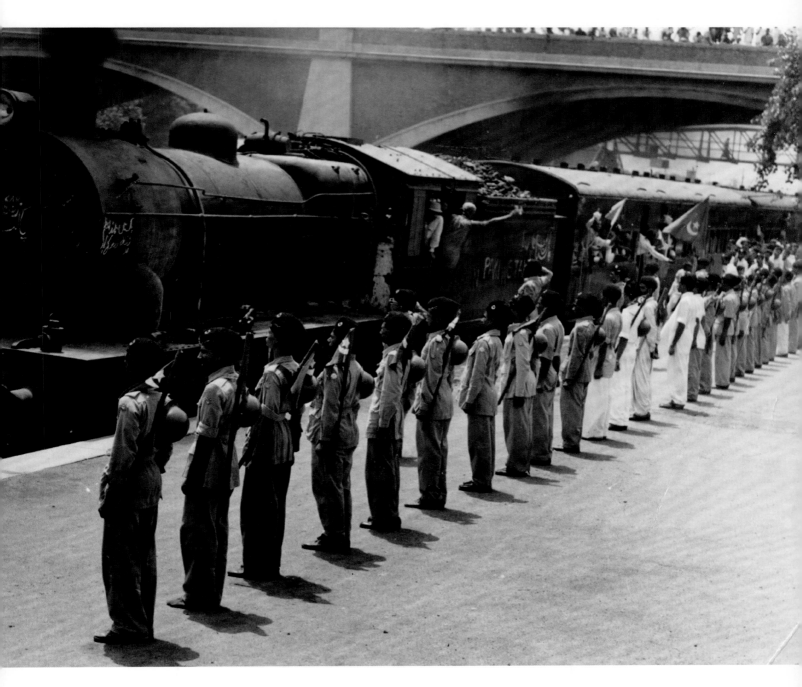

Stalin's communist regime then became very internalized and secretive, so that the USA and other Western nations became the Soviet Union's enemies in all but name. This state of affairs heightened with the more advanced development of nuclear weapons in the 1950s, so that the Cold War began. In essence, it was a diplomatic stalemate based on the premise of Mutually Assured Destruction (MAD) should a nuclear war ever breakout.

This situation perpetuated until 1991, when the Soviet Union collapsed. The countries of the Communist Bloc had their autonomy restored, as

did a fourteen other nations that had been under Soviet control since 1922. Russia remains the largest country in the world.

India, the single biggest British colony, was granted its independence in 1947. It coincided with the partitioning of the region according to religious differences, primarily Hindu and Muslim so that modern India and Pakistan were created. As the Hindus and Muslims were not neatly divided geographically prior to the partitioning, it resulted in a great deal of ethnic bloodshed as people were forcibly displaced and relocated by the process.

A poppy is left on a wall displaying the names of the missing on the Menin Gate Memorial, Ypres, Belgium

Index

Luftwaffe (German Air Force), 168, 180, 190, 214

Lynn, Vera, 225

Machine Gun Corps, 36

Manhattan Project, 291

Maquis, the (French Resistance), 204

Mata Hari (Margaretha Zelle), 123

Military Service Act, 1916, 20

mortar, 59, 61

Mussolini, Benito, 158, 237, 238

Mutually Assured Destruction (MAD), 299

Nagasaki, 291

Nazism, 106, 132, 145, 149, 161, 162, 166, 226, 228, 295, 296

North Africa Campaign, 195, 196

Nuremburg Trials, 296

Ohka, flying bomb, 288

Okinawa, 286, 288

Operation Braunschweig, 214

Operation Crossbow, 247, 248

Operation Overlord, 265, 268, 273

parachutes, 93

Pearl Harbor, 201, 202

Pershing, John, General,132, 135

Petain, Philippe, Marshall 204

Phony War, 166

Poland, invasion of, 156, 166, 188

POW, Japanese, 229, 230

POW, camps, 118, 120

Princip, Gavrilo, 13, 14

rationing, 183

Red Baron (Manfred von Richtofen), 117

Red Cross, 99, 118

Richtofen, Manfred von (Red Baron), 117

Rommel, Erwin, 266, 282

Royal Air Force (RAF), 42

Royal Army Dental Corps, 225

Royal Army Medical Corps, 225

Royal Flying Corps, 42

Royal Naval Air Service, 42

Russian Revolution, 27

Shell Crisis, 85

shell shock, 38

Stalin, Joseph, 160, 190, 297, 299

Stalingrad, Siege of, 212, 214

Stauffenberg, Claus von, 280

submarine, E-class, 50

Sudetenland, 156

Swinton, Ernest Dunlop, 52

tanks, 51, 52, 80, 88, 172, 174, 197

Third Reich, 135, 138, 204, 229, 237, 263, 273, 283

Treaty of Brest-Litovsk, 28

Treaty of Versailles, 132

trench foot, 22

trenches, 94, 95, 108, 111

Triple Entente, 15, 16, 72, 106

Tsar Nicholas, 27

Tunisia Campaign, 250, 252

U-boat, 48, 50, 206

V-weapons, 247, 248, 254, 275, 276

V.E. Day (Victory in Europe), 285

V.J. Day (Victory in Japan), 293

Vichy France, 204

Wall Street Crash, 149

war-dogs, 80

war-horses, 80

war-pigeons, 80

Western Front, 22. 27, 28, 31, 34, 41 45, 61, 65, 69, 72, 85, 87, 88, 90, 97, 102, 105, 108, 120, 212, 126, 274, 282

Women's Royal Air Force (WRAF), 223

Women's Royal Army Corps (WRAC), 223

Women's Royal Naval Service (WRNS), 223

Zeppelin, 57, 58

Zeppelin, Ferdinand von, Count, 57

Picture Credits

All images featured in this book are courtesy of Getty Images © Getty Images.

Page 292 - Alfred Eisenstaedt/Pix Inc./Time & Life Pictures/Getty Images